Few are living who remember the clashes of galloping raiders across the border ... The Hatfields and McCoys alike, as well as their neighbors whose ancestors had come into these rugged hills a hundred years before the feud days, have all come from the pioneer stock who pushed the frontier of civilization across the hills.

— Coleman A. Hatfield,
The City of Logan Centennial, 1952

4

The Feuding Hatfields & McCoys

Timeline And Pictorial History

Dr. Coleman C. Hatfield

with F. Keith Davis

Woodland Press, LLC

Woodland Press, LLC

Published by
WOODLAND PRESS, LLC
w w w . w o o d l a n d p r e s s . c o m

Copyright © 2012, Dr. Coleman C. Hatfield Family
ISBN 978-0-9793236-2-1
Now In Its Six Major Printing

SAN: 2 5 4 – 9 9 9 9

Introduction

AS A SCION of one of the feuding families of the Allegheny and Cumberland hills, and one whose forebearers began their trek westward from the Virginia coast, I offer the following for all who may be interested or desire to hear the facts from one who has first-hand knowledge of the people of whom he writes.

For many years those who best know me have beseeched me to give the public an authentic account of clan warfare in which my people were engaged. You *must* understand the minds of men of the hills who have been taught from childhood to suppress those matters of private concern among themselves, to employ every resource of their nature for the protection of themselves and their families.

Most who have read of the Hatfields and McCoys and their troubles during the last twenty years of the 19th century will say that the press, as well as all other biographers and historians, often placed the Hatfields in a less favorable light in the eyes of the world than the McCoys. I believe this estimate of public opinion has resulted from a lack of information regarding the true facts.

There has always been reluctance on the part of the Hatfields to air their troubles. Be conscious of the fact that the responsibility of such a fratricidal vendetta cannot be laid at the door of one side alone, but that each must bear the responsibility of his side of the cause insofar as that responsibility rests upon his shoulders.

This humble account depicts, in rather wide strokes with a timeline format, many of the family stories, facts and time periods pertaining to *The Feuding Hatfields & McCoys.*

Please withhold your judgment and make no decisions . . . until the last word has been read.

Dr. Coleman C. Hatfield
Great-Grandson of Anderson "Devil Anse" Hatfield
And Grandson of Cap Hatfield

Dr. Coleman C. Hatfield
1926 - 2008

The publishers of this book and the co-author would like to recognize and honor Dr. Coleman C. Hatfield for his research and passion in documenting his family's rich and colorful past. Besides being a gifted student of history and an accomplished author, he was a dear friend.

We've been careful in this volume to ensure that it is presented in Dr. Hatfield's unique and distinct voice, and offered with his entertaining Appalachian storytelling flair.

Here you'll find a timeline of events that tracks the history of the Hatfield migration westward in broad strokes, and eventually meanders its way to the rich American story of the Hatfield & McCoy Feud. It's coupled with a variety of unique family stories that have been passed down through the children of Anderson "Devil Anse" Hatfield. To complete this effort, two final, pertinent chapters have been included: one by Dr. Hatfield's father, C.A. Hatfield, and another by Logan County journalist and historian G.T. Swain.

It's our hope that this volume—along with Dr. Hatfield's earlier work, *The Tale Of The Devil*—will live up to his vision and honor his legacy as an Appalachian historian.

It's now time to turn the page. May the contents of this book encourage each reader to investigate and document his or her own family stories and keep this type of history alive for the benefit of future generations.

—F. Keith Davis

Table Of Contents

Chapter One
Early American Overview

Genealogical records show that William Hatfield landed in Southampton, Virginia, in 1622. In subsequent years, up to 1638, he was granted certain acreage in Southampton in remuneration for his having paid transportation from England to the Colonies for numerous immigrants.

Documentation also shows that in 1626, in James City, Virginia, Joseph Hatfield petitioned, as a free man along with others, to leave his barren farmland and an "utterly decayed house" and move onto better areas — greener pastures.

The year was 1633 and Joseph Hatfield, planter, leased acreage in Elizabeth City County, Virginia, bordering on the Southampton River. Wills and other documents that have been registered and discovered in Southampton prove that the Hatfields stayed in this area for a number of generations.

However, facts also indicate that the descendants of immigrant Joseph Hatfield followed the Wilderness Road, which led from Richmond, Virginia, to the picturesque mountains of southwest Virginia, eastern Kentucky and eastern Tennessee.

1770 — Captain Andrew Hatfield appears in the Botetourt County, Virginia, records.

1773 — It is known that Fort Hatfield, Giles County, Virginia, was built and maintained by Captain Andrew Hatfield as an outpost to guard against Indian depredations. The place where the fort originally stood is still called the Hatfield voting precinct.

Oct. 10, 1774 — Captain Thomas Burk and Andrew Hatfield, then a member of his company, engage in the significant Battle of Point Pleasant: the first battle of the American Revolution.

1773-1797 — "Revolutionary" Joseph Hatfield, brother to Captain Andrew Hatfield from pension records in Russell County, Virginia, showed outstanding service and a courageous spirit during the American Revolution: Private and Indian spy of the Virginia Militia under Colonel Chrisman, serving two campaigns of six months.

Testimony also stated that Joseph was considered "the best spy and woodsman of that part of the country" and was "always chosen by his officers." His duty under Captain Scott was three tours of three months each; under Captain Campbell, two tours of three months each; and a period of time under Captain Lyle and Captain Sevier, between 1778 and 1782.

"Revolutionary" Joseph, who was a widower, and his son, Ephraim, age nine at the signing of the Declaration of Independence, migrated to Russell County, Virginia, right before the Revolution. It was in 1779 that Joseph, age 39, married young, 18-year-old Rachael Smith. Rachael and Joseph never had children of their own, but Rachael became the stepmother to Ephraim, then 14 years old.

It was around this time that Joseph and Rachael moved to Campbell County, Tennessee, where Joseph eventually passed away in 1832. It was from Rachael's petition for Joseph's pension in 1841 that we have records of his service during the Revolution. Rachael received the sum of $80.00 per annum until her death in 1851.

1785-1790 — Ephraim Hatfield, who was born in 1765, married Mary Goff Smith, a widow with a son, Tom. Mary was the sister-in-law to Eph's stepmother, Rachael. Both were twenty at the time of their marriage and had four children by 1790: Joseph, born (b.) 1787 (named after his paternal grandfather); Ericus, b. 1788 (named after his maternal grandfather); Valentine, b. 1789 (through whom we follow the direct line of descent); and Bridget, b. 1790. There is no record as to the date or reason of Mary Smith Hatfield's death; however, it is presumed she died in childbirth with her last child. Ephraim became a widower at age 25 and was responsible for raising four babies.

Chapter Two
The Tap Root

This volume traces its true, direct line back to Ephraim Hatfield, known by the West Virginia or feuding Hatfields as Eph-of-All, and his son Valentine. It's through a very exciting series of events that Eph-of-All came to remarry and take his new family from Russell County, Virginia, on to Pike County, Kentucky.

1792 — This was the time when certain foreign agents of the Great Lakes country, where their hold had not been relinquished, were offering gunpowder and bullets for the scalps of settlers who were coming through the backdoor of western Virginia in a determined advance to settle the land of the Northwest Territory. The bloody mercenaries used the Indians to attack the Virginia settlements of the New River and Clinch Valleys (Old Andrew's Fort in Giles County was built to protect settlers and wagon trains from such attacks).

On August 12, 1792, the cabin home of David Musick, on Thompson's Creek, in Russell County, was assaulted by a vicious band of Shawnee Indians (See The Tragic Death of David Musick). Brave David fell guarding the threshold of his home. He was simply charged and overwhelmed by the number of Shawnee. Thereafter, his wife and children were carried away into captivity, but soon were overtaken and rescued at Haysi, Dickinson County, by a party of white frontiersmen who were seasoned in the ways of the American Indians of the region.

The Tragic Death Of David Musick

On August 12, 1792, David Musick lived on what was then the frontier on

12

Thompson Creek, Russell County, Virginia. Early in the morning of that day his home was besieged by a band of Shawnee American Indians. Their headquarters was in the Scioto Valley far away in Ohio Territory. Two of the boys had gone out to gather wood for the fire when they discovered the savages skulking nearby, ready for a dash toward the cabin. The children return quickly and the father directed that the doors be barred while he undertook to load his flintlock.

As the Indians charged upon the house, Musick had difficulty with his rifle. As he had his weapon in place, his wife brought a bit of fire from the fireplace embers in an effort to ignite the powder in the loading pan on the breech of the old gun, but the fire failed and an arrow from one of the redmen critically wounded Musick.

The Indians immediately sprang upon him with their tomahawks and he was brutally murdered and mutilated in the presence of his terrified wife and children. The Indians then carried Musick's widow, Anna, and their five children away.

Before leaving the premises they had trouble catching one of the Musick family horses, which was running loose in the pasture. After surrounding the animal they "creased" the neck of the horse with an arrow and then had no trouble bringing it under control. They also butchered a steer. After removing the skin, the Indians made a bag out of the hide and filled it with the best parts of the beef and loaded this improvised bag on a horse and set the oldest boy on the horse and got ready for the journey back to Ohio land.

The oldest son was a bright twelve-year-old with a head full of red hair. The Indians looked upon him with favor as they seemingly dreamed of adopting him into their tribe as a future chief. Perhaps this was, in part, because of his unusual hair color.

The Indians ate the meat from the freshly killed beef without cooking it and required the poor mother and her children to take raw meat and eat it for their nourishment, as well. The smallest child of the Musick family, a five-year-old boy, cried and refused to eat raw meat, whereupon one of the savages cruelly grasped the child and jammed his face against a rough tree causing lacerations that left lifetime scars on the boy's face.

An elderly man who lived nearby became aware of the raid on the Musick home and ran a number of miles to the next neighbor, but, being overcome with exhaustion and fright, he collapsed dead at the doorway. Yet, just before he died he was able to murmur a few words about the fate of the Musick clan. The awful news spread throughout the settlement and a posse of armed white men gathered and set out in pursuit of the Indians.

The savages, believing their presence was unknown to other settlers, camped on an island near the present site of Haysi, in Dickinson County, Virginia. The Musicks overheard one Indian who was able to speak broken English say they would camp on the island, where "no white man come here." However, the determined posse of frontiersmen discovered the camping party at daybreak on the following day.

The brave widow, seeing her rescuers approaching, grabbed her smallest child and dashed toward the posse. An Indian hurled his tomahawk barely missing her and the child as they ran. In the skirmish that ensued, the white settlers killed one of the Indians and the others fled into the forest.

It is not known whether Ephraim Hatfield was one of the members of the rescue posse or not; however, this is a distinct possibility since all of the men of the settlement were bound in a common cause of defense of their homes. They must, of necessity, stand side by side in defense of their loved ones, and thus it is seen from the earliest beginning of our history that the common defense and the general welfare of all neighbors was guarded by the settlers even to the most remote mountain recesses as the frontier line moved westward.

From this time, whatever may have been the dramatic event that brought

Ephraim and Anna together, they both, having the care and the future of their respective offspring at heart, became interested in each other and later married.

As Coleman A. Hatfield wrote in a 1952 article:

Sometime after the rescue of the Musick family, Ephraim Hatfield and the widow, Anna Musick, were married and, like many other sturdy pioneers, set out to with their families across the mountain toward the Sandy River country, and settled on Blackberry Creek in Pike County, Kentucky, not many miles from the present city of Matewan, West Virginia.

This romance, between Ephraim and Anna, is where the story of one of the feud families of the Kentucky-West Virginia border really begins.

Chapter Three
Ephraim Marries A Widow

1802 — The young widower, Ephraim Hatfield, later married the widow of David Musick, of Thompson's Creek, and they set out to cross the blue hills in the West headed for the Sandy River Valley, which was the borderline of the great newly created state of Kentucky. It was upon the soil of this state that Ephraim and Anna Musick Hatfield first built their home on the Blackberry Fork of the Tug River, sixty years before the first shot of the Civil War.

1812 — Valentine Hatfield serves in the War of 1812 under Captain Burwell Spurlock. He later became known as "Wall" Hatfield, and settled on Tug River at the present site of Sprigg in the county of Mingo. "Uncle Wally," as he was known in later years, reared his family of twelve children, among whom was the second Ephraim.

Late author and Logan County historian Robert Y. Spence once described Valentine's role as one of the early settlers in Virginia (now West Virginia): "On Gilbert Creek, one of the first settlers was Isaac Spratt, who built a home on a survey made for Edward Crawford. Frederick Trent also built a home there about 1806, and other pioneers of that section were Thomas Smith and Valentine Hatfield."

1813 — Ephraim and Anna move their family of nine children at the suggestion of Ephraim's stepson, Tom Smith, who had traveled extensively through the lush mountains of Kentucky. Ephraim and his family drop from census records as of this date. It was also in this year that young Ericus, or Ale, Hatfield dies from a self-inflicted wound while trying to bleed a deer while out hunting. He dies before he can reach aid.

Eph and Anna had children of their own: George, b. 1804; Jeremiah, b. 1809; and several other female children. Valentine Hatfield, born in 1789, and his wife, Martha Weddington, settled on the Tug River in what is now West Virginia and had twelve children: Ale, b. 1804; Joseph, b. 1806; Ephraim, b. 1811; twins John and Andrew, b. 1813; Thomas, b. 1818; Jacob, b. 1819; James, b. 1824; Valentine, b. 1831; and daughters, Virginia, Phoebe and Celia (or Sena or Cena).

1820 — Eph-of-All and son, Valentine, visit Russell County.

1826 — Ephraim, born in 1811, is known in this manuscript as Big Eph and eventually marries Nancy Vance, who was born in 1813. The direct line of descent continues through their son Anderson Hatfield, their third son who was later known as "Devil Anse," born 1839.

In the book *The Tale Of The Devil*, this is how the Devil's birth was described: Nancy Vance Hatfield, the mother of Anderson Hatfield, went into childbirth on September 9, 1839, at the log cabin home she shared with her husband, Ephraim Hatfield, on the Straight Fork of Mate Creek, a tributary of the Tug Fork of the Big Sandy River which marked the border of western Virginia — today's West Virginia — and Kentucky. It is likely that Nancy Hatfield was attended by at least one midwife, known in popular usage as a "granny woman." Ansie, as the boy was also nicknamed, was the fifth child in Ephraim and Nancy's growing family, preceded by John in 1829, Valentine in 1834, Elizabeth in 1836, and Martha in 1838. During the following twenty years, Ephraim and Nancy would have six other children: Ellison in 1842, Elias in 1848, Emma in 1849, Biddie in 1850, and twins Smith and Patterson in 1854. The oldest boy, John, died in 1841, at age twelve.

Chapter Four

Logan Wildcats, Nation Divided

A significant date in Hatfield family history is April 19, 1861, the day when Anderson "Devil Anse" Hatfield married Louvicey "Vicey" Chafin, who was born in 1842. Not long after making his wedding vows with Louvicey, Anse picks up his long rifle and joins the Confederacy.

Nancy Hatfield once recalled:

My boy, Ansie, was captain of all the soldiers from Beech to Mate. When the war was about to start, they were practicing being soldiers among the home guards on the other side over in Kentucky, and Ansie and two other neighbor boys, Mose Chafin and Davie Mounts, went over to watch them march where General Bill France had men on Peter Creek.

General Bill said our boys were spies. When Virginia seceded, General Bill said to Ansie, "Look at the shape your state is in." He made one of his men fight Ansie, and my boy got the best of him. Then he set another man on Ansie, and my boy then downed the second man.

Then General Bill told his company to drive our boys back across the river into Virginia. They threw rocks at Ansie and Mose and Davie. They had to run to keep from being killed because General Bill had fifty men or more. This caused a whole lot of trouble because all of the boys on our side of the river were terribly mad at the way General Bill's soldiers had treated them.

1856-1860 — Devil Anse, a courageous and loyal Rebel, is eventually named captain of the famous "Logan Wildcats," and is responsible for bringing men of his territory to central training twice each year. It was this local militia, under General John B. Floyd and his brother Colonel George H. C. Floyd, that volunteered their various skills to the Southern cause.

The raw abilities of Devil Anse were many, as were those of most of the butternuts from the region. He was well suited for the local armed band, being he was an expert horseman, exceptional rifle shot, and experienced hunter. Most men from the area were fine trackers who were able to move through the Appalachian woodlands with an amazing degree of stealth. This was especially so with Devil Anse Hatfield since he was raised "in the deepest part of the hills" of Appalachia. He was weaned on trapping, hunting and creatively living off the land.

Oddly enough, Randall "Ran'l" McCoy and Anderson "Devil Anse" Hatfield are neighbors by the outbreak of the War Between the States. Author Truda Williams McCoy gave some description of the McCoy patriarch in her book, *The McCoys: Their Story*:

> (Randall) had a standard of right and wrong — a code which he lived by. He believed in God and the Devil. No man in his right mind could doubt the Devil , not after he had lived as close to the Hatfields as he had.

Randall, being too old to join the confederate forces, sympathized with the Southern cause, contrary to the views of many of his neighbors and relatives, including Harmon McCoy, his own blood brother, who was a soldier under General Bill France and the Home Guards of Kentucky.

Devil Anse and the hundreds of other mountain fathers and sons suffer under ever-increasing pressure to return to their homes for several reasons:

> 1. - To provide protection against marauders from both sides who raided family farms for fresh horses, cattle and supplies;
> 2. - to do the seasonal planting and harvesting to provide for their families;

3. - and to return home from a "six-month tour" that had actually lasted three long years.

August 6th, 1862 — The Battle of Beech Creek, or Battle of Devil's Backbone, in Logan County took place. Single-handedly, Devil Anse Hatfield holds off a troop of Union Soldiers as the sole rifleman makes it appear that many are firing down from a rocky ridge. It is not known whether Devil Anse lent his name to this ridge or took his nick-name "Devil" from this victorious battle.

1863 — Two events lead to Captain Devil Anse Hatfield's failure to answer muster on Sept. 1, 1863. This year includes the death of General John B. Floyd, who Devil Anse had served under in the Logan Wildcats, going back to 1856, years before joining the Confederacy.

August 1863 — After the Battle of Gettysburg and Lee's retreat southward, Devil Anse is ordered by General Beckley to execute Slayter Jim Hatfield and Anse Toler (a Hatfield in-law) for desertion.

Fall 1863 — After several assassination attempts instigated by General Bill France of the Kentucky Home Guard failed against Devil Anse, Ran'l McCoy, Confederate sympathizer and friend of Devil Anse, along with a band of men, meet with Devil Anse on a secret mission. McCoy offers to lead Devil Anse to a strategic position in the territory where General Bill France is returning from his main headquarters to his home on Peter Creek, in Pike County.

The group eventually surrounds France's home and Devil Anse fires on the general, wounding him. The rebs then charge and capture the general for interrogation. The killing of General Bill, through the combined efforts of Ran'l and Devil Anse and their followers, arouses the Home Guards of Kentucky.

Harmon McCoy, brother to Ran'l, takes up an assassination assignment and attempts to shoot Devil Anse one wintry night as he lay with fever at his home. Missing the shot and a perfect opportunity, Harmon flees into the mountains to hide. Anse' wife, Louvicey, alerts Captain Jim Vance and Jim Wheeler Wilson, who then track down McCoy and kill him not far from his secluded hideout.

Thus starts the hard feelings between the McCoys and Hatfields; and, before long, the McCoy family blames Devil Anse for the political differences between Ran'l and Harmon. Of course, they subsequently blame Devil Anse for Harmon's death.

Devil Anse Hatfield

21

Chapter Five
Death Of Toler's Wife

In August of 1863, General Alfred Beckley's army was encamped in east Tennessee. Many of his men had been recruited from the southern section of what is now West Virginia, having followed their general from the little home city bearing his name, which is located on top of the rolling hills of the Flat Top mountains. His soldiers are the ancestors of hundreds of descendants who now live in the foothills of the Alleghenies in the southern region of the Mountain State. Among his soldiers were Anse Toler and Slayter Jim Hatfield, brothers-in-law from Wyoming County.

Beckley's army was poised for action, guarding Lee's backdoor, ready to join his forces in combating the Union Army as it was breaking through the Cumberlands in a determined effort to roll across the plains of Georgia to the sea. All leaves were cancelled as Beckley stated that no man could be spared at such a critical moment.

A message came to Anse Toler that his wife, who was back in the hills, was at the point of death and not expected to live. Toler felt that he needed a friend to approach General Beckley at such a serious moment. No one in the outfit was better suited or more willing to request a favor for any of his men than Lieutenant Anderson Hatfield, then a young soldier who was tough as a hickory and always ready for action. One writer has since described Anderson: "… six feet of devil and 180 pounds of hell, and yet he had a generous heart and kindly face, flowing hair that curled upward, as it reached near his shoulders. Nothing escaped his searching brown eyes. His broke down [sic] nose, which was described by one as a 'Wellington beak,' stood prominent above his fine suit of coffee brown beard. He was looked upon as a friend and buddy to every one of the boys in grey. No one else among the hill people was ever found with a personality so full of perseverance, as well as self-reliance and confidence in his own ability to obtain aid and comfort for those who trusted in his leadership. The energetic young lieutenant approached his commanding officer and appealed to him to permit Anse Toler and Slayter Jim to go to the family bedside of Toler's wife. The request was promptly rejected."

Hatfield—who always said, "blood is thicker than water," and with no authority from his superiors—quietly called his two buddies out and permitted them to go on their mission, promising that he would stand between them and all danger when they returned. The soldiers were escorted through the north lines of the army and rode toward Anse Toler's cabin in the hills of Wyoming County, West Virginia, where his dying wife awaited his return.

When he reached her bedside she opened her failing eyes and said, "I knowed God would bring you to me, Ansy, before I died. I couldn't bear to leave the children until you were here. I'm so glad that Jim came with you. Sister Rachel will be able to bear it much better knowing that both of you were here when I went home to Jesus."

The grief-stricken soldier stood by and watched his neighbors and kinsmen lay the body of his wife to rest, and after telling the children good-bye for awhile, Toler and Slayter Jim mounted their horses to ride day and night until they came again to General Beckley's command.

The stern old southerner speedily called a court martial and after reviewing the circumstances, ordered Anderson Toler and James Hatfield to be shot at sunrise on the following day. Inconsistent as it may seem in the face of all that happened, he called Lieutenant Hatfield and directed him to execute the condemned men at daybreak on the following morning. The grim-faced young officer muttered as he strode out of the headquarters of General Beckley, that if Toler and Slayter Jim had to die that many more would bite the dust.

Just across the valley General Henry Witcher, the Confederate raider of the black flag, was encamped with his army. Under his command was Old Capt. Jim Vance of Russell County, a maternal uncle to Capt. Anderson Hatfield. A secret message was dispatched by Hatfield to Jim, the message being carried by Henry Mitchell, one of Witcher's men, and sent to Old Jim Vance, requesting him to bring forty of his best horses, saddles, and bridles for the use of Hatfield in carrying out a detailed order of General Beckley.

As the dawn lifted over the Cumberlands on the following morning, forty grey clad soldiers mounted on as many of the best of Witcher's horses, riding in a sweeping gallop northward up the Clinch River Valley through southwest Virginia, their hard haunches beating forty Buena Vista saddles, the ill gotten gain of Witcher, of the black flag, who always took horses but never any prisoners. At the front of this column rode Anse Toler and Slayter Jim (having been saved from the firing squad by a daring, pre-dawn shoot-'em-up rescue). Next behind, with his eyes never wavering from the condemned soldiers, Capt. Devil Anse Hatfield led the remainder of the speeding column. The intrepid, brown-bearded soldier with the so-called Wellington beak, leaving the "lost cause," rode back to the new state that only a short time before had joined the Union.

1865 – The Civil War comes to and end and Abraham Lincoln is assassinated at Ford Theatre in Washington D.C. The 13th Amendment abolishes slavery.

1867 – Congress approves legislation that allows blacks to vote in the District of Columbia.

Chapter Six
The Sow And Piglets

For more than ten years after the Civil War, Devil Anse Hatfield and Ran'l McCoy lived in peace. McCoy owned a large track of land on Blackberry and Pond Fork just over in Pike County, Kentucky. Devil Anse, after returning from the Civil War, took up 5,000 acres of virgin timber in West Virginia.

Mountain soldiers came back to their rundown farms with determination to build up or recover what they had lost in the way of horses, cattle and other livestock, or start over if they must, and with strong determination to stand guard over their families. The enmity of neighbors had to be overcome. Terrible grudges and ill will resulting from the fratricidal conflict had set back law and order; hard sentiment had grown up between different communities and families.

1878 — Argument over Sow and Piglets: It seems that every household throughout the mountains has herds of swine that roam the hills freely in autumn eating and growing fat on forest growth. Every family herd has its own hog mark, a specific manner of cutting or notching the ears. All of these various combinations of markings are made by each owner and easily recognized by all as the property of the owner whose mark was known throughout the countryside.

A sow, thus marked, and her piglets were caught and penned by Floyd Hatfield who lived across the creek from Ran'l McCoy. Both men claim ownership and McCoy appeals to Valentine "Wall" Hatfield, Justice of the Peace, for a summons to determine ownership in court.

Floyd Hatfield

Justice Hatfield disqualifies himself, for obvious reasons, and the case goes before Squire Stafford and testimony is heard for a day and a half. The testimony as to ownership is evenly split until Bill Staton, brother-in-law to Floyd Hatfield, takes the stand. With commanding demeanor, while glaring at McCoy's sons who had played some prank on him in the past, Staton testifies that he saw Floyd mark this sow. The judgment goes against McCoy for insufficient proof of ownership.

Spring 1879 — Sam and Paris McCoy, while hoeing corn on the West Virginia side of the river, jump Bill Staton as he rides by the cornfield. Indeed, Staton may have been looking for trouble himself; it was reported that Sam McCoy held the bridle while Paris pulled Staton to the ground. In the attack, Paris is wounded and Staton killed. Ellison Hatfield, brother to Devil Anse and brother-in-law to Staton, takes an active part in apprehending the McCoys and bringing them to trial. The McCoy boys are sent to prison and Ran'l McCoy swears vengeance.

March 1879 — Meanwhile, across the country, New Mexico Governor Lew Wallace (the future author of *Ben Hur*) made out a list of desperados he wanted arrested in Lincoln County, New Mexico. The list included such Wild West notables as Texas John Slaughter and Billy the Kid (Kid Antrum).

Chapter Seven
Mountain Romeo And Juliet

1879 — Christmas Eve Frolic — Young men and women from all over attend a dance at the home of the Maynard family on Lick Creek. Young men tote pistols and whiskey; frequent fist fights result as sympathies lingering from Civil War days divide the young men into groups. The Hatfield boys, specifically Johnse and Cap, attend and get into a fight. Cap is seriously wounded in the kidney and lower colon but miraculously survives. Johnse, rumored to be operating a still, is known for his fiery disposition because of his drinking and his inclination to "throw his weight around;" and due to his good looks (bright-haired, fair-faced, blue-eyed Johnse), he was known throughout the mountains as a "ladies man." Johnson Hatfield had built quite a reputation by the time he reached twenty.

Election August 1880 — Young people congregated and met through frolics, religious revival meetings (so-called "sociations") and at elections. Although Johnson "Johnse" Hatfield may have met and spoken with Roseanne McCoy, age 22, prior to the Pikeville election, it was at this time the couple defy their families and go away to share many private hours.

Matthew Hatfield, a Kentucky Hatfield, was up for sheriff of Pikeville and asked his cousins from West Virginia to assist Preacher Anse Hatfield, Justice of the Peace, at the voting headquarters. Johnse' mother, Louvicey, worries about her son's propensity for drink and fightin' and about his eye for Roseanne McCoy. Since drink is not allowed at the polling place, the Hatfield boys drink all the way to the election, and then take up their guns and ride over to Pikeville. Ran'l McCoy is just as concerned: there is usually fightin' due to the nature of politics, and this is a Hatfield election. He also worries about his daughter, Roseanne; she and Johnson Hatfield "seem to

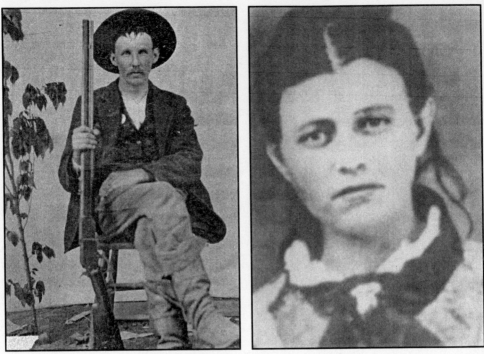

Johnse Hatfield and Roseanna McCoy

manage to get together." McCoy warns his family and Roseanne rides to town on the back of her brother's horse.

Sometime during the day, Johnsie and Roseanne steal off together and are not missed until Ran'l discovers Tolbert returning home late at night without Roseanne.

Johnse takes Roseanne home but they are not given permission to marry. Finding herself unwelcome at the Hatfield homestead and also in her own home, Roseanne goes to live with Uncle Jim Vance's family and she and Johnse continue to see one another. She later moves to her Aunt Betty's home in Stringtown and continues to see Johnse for about a year after their elopement. [The manuscript reports that the McCoy family repeatedly asks Roseanne to move home but she refuses so that she can continue to see Johnse; other sources report that Ran'l McCoy refuses to take his daughter back into his home yet repeatedly tries to keep Johnse from seeing her.]

Christmas Eve 1881 — Frolic at Maynard home, Lick Creek – Ran'l and his sons, Tolbert, Dick, Floyd and Buddy find Johnse with Roseanne. They "arrest" Johnse for carrying a gun and proceed to tie him and take him to jail. Roseanne disappears during the commotion and finds a horse; she rides quickly through the night over the snow-covered mountains to alert Devil Anse. Devil Anse, his brother, Elias, and six other Hatfields intercept the McCoys. Both groups dismount and exchange bitter dialogue — the most bitter words that these two mountain leaders had ever exchanged. Ran'l spared no words in his denunciation of young Johnse. Devil Anse countered with recriminating accusations against Randall and his set as troublemakers.

There is truly no one final version to the rest of this ill-fated pair's story. Roseanne was indeed pregnant with Johnse' child, but there are at least four versions concerning it:

1. - *Roseanne miscarried the baby after her long and traumatic ride over the mountains.*
2. - *She miscarried the child after contracting fever and measles.*
3. - *She delivered a girl child named Sallie after her mother whom she greatly missed.*
4. - *She delivered a son she named Johnson.*

Roseanne's death shortly after the 1881 frolic is believed to be due to pneumonia coupled with heartbreak over her father's embittered and unforgiving attitude. Another version relates how she died from deep anguish over the death of her daughter of nine months. Another explanation is that she died of heartbreak over the eventual marriage of Johnse to her cousin, Nancy McCoy — daughter to Harmon McCoy.

1882 — Johnse married Nancy McCoy. They have two children: "Anse the Older" and Stella.

Chapter Eight
Election Day Horror

Aug. 5, 1882 — Pikeville Election: Matthew Hatfield, again up for re-election, requests help of his West Virginia cousins, Elias and Ellison Hatfield. Old Ran'l McCoy is in town with his sons, Tolbert, Randolph "Buddy" Jr., Floyd, Calvin and Pharmer.

At 4:00 p.m., Tolbert McCoy and Elias Hatfield get into a fight over a debt and Ellison, unarmed, tries to mediate. Tolbert, Pharmer and Buddy descend on the 6-foot Ellison Hatfield, stabbing him 26 times and shooting him in the back. Sheriff Matthew, trying to come to Ellison's aid, is wounded. Horrified bystanders finally come between the fighters and disarm the McCoys. Several men mount their horses riding to tell friends and family and to summon Ellison's wife. Ellison, gravely wounded, is carried to West Virginia to the home of a relative where his pregnant wife and young children join him. Preacher Anse Hatfield, fearing immediate retaliation from the West Virginia Hatfields, tries to convince Ran'l McCoy that his sons would be safer in the jail at the county seat 35 miles away. Devil Anse Hatfield, gathering his own posse, decides to administer his own form of mountain justice and rides into Kentucky.

April 3, 1882 — To put the time period in perspective, Jesse James, alias Thomas Howard, is shot and killed by Bob Ford while he straightened a picture on the wall of his rented home in Saint Joseph, Missouri.

August 7, 1882 — Preacher Anse Hatfield and other Hatfield lawmen escort the prisoners and their father toward Pikeville. Overtaken by Valentine and Elias Hatfield, the posse is convinced to turn back. Devil Anse and his family are headed toward Pikeville to overtake the prisoners. On their way back, Devil Anse surrounds and takes the three boys away from the law-

men. Devil Anse takes the boys to an abandoned schoolhouse in West Virginia to hold them until he knows whether Ellison will live or die.

Through August 13, 1882, Sarah McCoy and her daughters repeatedly appeal to Devil Anse to release the boys to the law.

"Big" Jim McCoy and thirty-eight men ride on to the homes of Devil Anse and Cap Hatfield; yet, the two groups of armed men do not encounter one another.

Ran'l McCoy rides on to the county seat of Pikeville, to appeal to a higher authority to save his boys.

August 14, 1882 — Ellison Hatfield dies; the boys are taken out, tied to trees and shot. The gunshots are reportedly heard throughout the community.

Ran'l McCoy was unable to get anyone from Pikeville to travel into the mountains to intercede with mountain justice, not that this help would have been in time. Ran'l never saw his sons alive again.

Chapter Nine
Story Of Mob Rule

Then appeared on the border Professor Charles C. Carpenter. Nobody seemed to know whence he came and only a few hints were ever learned of his past. For his exceptional breadth of learning and ability there had been no one to surpass him in keenness of intellect, and he made many friends in the young group of mountaineers who flocked to him and listened as he taught them in the subjects such as they had never learned before.

Grown young men and women also learned to read and write under his tutelage, but there was another side to this red-haired stranger. Charlie was in his early forties with large tiger-like, searching eyes that, even when he was busily engaged, would often "eye-ball" the roadways in the distance as if he expected to be surprised and would turn quickly as if he sensed danger. Patrons often stated, "Professor Carpenter was plenty smart."

Besides his gift as an educator, he had other skills, as well. He was a crack-shot. He could take a rifle and shoot the walnuts out of a tree without missing; he also kept a .38 concealed under his coat or loose-fitting shirt, but only a few ever knew about it. He confided to two or three of the older boys of the school that he had been shot at every year since the Civil War.

Here our educator, or agitator, was the organizer and instigator of a terrible dangerous act of mob violence.

Mob rule hardly ever gets out of hand over any situation without some leader who sparks the movement and without this unorganized, unthinking, potentially dangerous destructive force, it would never be released or get under way.

During the time of stress and excitement, Charlie C. Carpenter was busily going about among the men and boys spreading his insidious plans of hate and murder.

He spoke to groups of these disillusioned mountain men behind the old log school house where he had counseled the youth of the neighborhood, and in which there was quartered the three McCoy brothers. Carpenter drew up a document containing a set of resolutions and summoned mostly young men together at midnight where a lighted pine torch was driven in a stump in their midst and read to them:

"… Now, therefore, be it resolved that there shall be a summary action to put an end to murder and violence and that we hereby agree to stand together in all that we do for the protection for ourselves and other citizens of this territory, and that the guilty be punished according to their deeds, an eye for an eye and a tooth for a tooth, and that all other things which be just and proper be done for the good of our community…"

By the red glare of the flickering pine torches Charlie harangued the crowd of approximately thirty young men and boys gathered around to hear the reading of his resolutions.

Many of the older men disagreed and failed to attend the meeting which they suspected of being wrong, but this convincing mob leader, Charlie C. Carpenter, whose subtle argument and persuasive entreaties carried out the murderous plot and Tolbert, Dick (Pharmer) and young Randall "Buddy" McCoy were taken across to the Kentucky side of the river and murdered without judge or jury and without due process of law.

Be it said to the praise of Tolbert and Dick that they begged for the life of their young brother, 15, and offered Charlie that if the boy could be spared that they would willingly die for the crime that he committed. The unrelenting mob leader would not consider their last request.

Less than twenty-four hours after the McCoy brothers were shot down, the tall professor was last seen crossing the hill southward, and was never seen again in those parts.

Thus we have an illustration of illiterate men whose names had to be signed by their mark "X" being lead by an educated criminal whose bloody trail, no doubt, extended along the many frontiers where he had inculcated evil and hatred in the minds of those he taught.

Perhaps this was the reason that he sought a change of climate and, perhaps, it can be well understood why he had been shot at every year for 17 years following the close of the Civil War. Old Doc Redeford said, "They must have had bad marksmen in the places where Charlie Carpenter traveled!"

Chapter Ten
Bounty Hunters

September 1882 — Ran'l McCoy obtains indictments against twenty men in the murder of his sons, issued through Judge Brown, Pike County. Warrants are also issued for witnesses to the crime.

February 1883 — There are no arrests to date. At this time, the Hatfields withdraw from the Kentucky-West Virginia border and buy lands from Old Hawk Steele and family who are moving west.

1883 - 1885 — Border warfare between the feuding families has reached such proportions that the McCoy clan besiege Governor Simon B. Buckner to offer rewards for the extradition of the Hatfields from West Virginia to Kentucky. Like action is taken by Emanuel W. Wilson, Governor of West Virginia, for certain members of the McCoy clan who are charged with crimes in West Virginia. (It should be noted that neither Governor honors the extradition papers of the other state.)

This standstill lasts for six years; many attempts are made by various bounty hunters and "detectives" to kidnap various Hatfield and McCoy family members and literally drag them across the state borders where warrants will be honored and bounties paid.

Meanwhile, "yellow journalism" sensationalizes and exaggerates the feud across the nation and attracts bounty hunters nationwide.

1885 — Cap and Johnse travel to Charleston, West Virginia, and receive assurances from Governor Wilson that if raids across the Tug River against the Hatfields continued, he would send militia to patrol the southern boundary of the state. At the same time, he cautions them against raids by Hatfield family members into Kentucky.

The Battle of Grapevine Creek: rumors reach the Hatfields that the Mc-

Coys are coming in great numbers. The Hatfields barricade themselves on Grapevine Creek in clear view of the Kentucky hills. Ammunition and instructions are given to a group of McCoys by Pikeville Sheriff Dick Murphy and prosecuting attorney, Perry Cline.

Two young girls are sent out by Louvicey to warn her husband, Devil Anse, and his men. The girls are apprehended and threatened by Big Jim McCoy and Deputy Frank Phillips for information. The Hatfields re-route the McCoys when they separate the McCoys from their horses. One McCoy is wounded. In the flight from West Virginia, Deputy Phillips fires upon the home of Cap Hatfield and brutally kills Billy Dempsey, a cousin of the nationally renowned prize-fighter, Jack Dempsey.

During the political campaign of 1887, Ran'l McCoy approaches his brother-in-law, Perry Cline, district attorney of Pike County, Kentucky, concerning the extradition of certain Hatfields. Extending campaign promises to the McCoy family, Cline approaches the governor of Kentucky who issues extradition papers. These are handed to Deputy Phillips, a person who himself is indicted in West Virginia for the murder of innocent persons and illegal raids into that state.

In December 1887, Johnson Hatfield and his Kentucky attorney meet with Perry Cline at the Kentucky Court House. The Hatfield family pays Cline $225.00 to cease extradition proceedings (Cline's expenses). Both state governors are enraged that such an arrangement should be entered into and Kentucky Governor Buckner even addresses his general assembly on the subjection on December 31, 1887.

Chapter Eleven
Pushboats Bring
Merchandise to the Hills

During the last quarter of the nineteenth century, the period with which we are most concerned, and particularly before rail traffic had come into the hill country, steamboats from the Ohio and the Big Sandy came up to Catlettsburg, Fort Gay and Louisa; but these steam vessels were unable to ascend the rapids of the Tug Fork and east of Louisa. It was here that the pushboat traffic took over. There were many engaged in pushboat shipping with boats seventy to eighty feet in length and eight feet in width. The business of bringing manufactured goods upstream, as well as moving families, their household goods, ginseng and other products from the upper reaches of the stream, became a business within its own and employed several boatmen.

The boats were loaded at the Big Sandy towns and a crew of ten was allotted to each boat. When the boats were loaded, it took four men to each side with the long spike poles with shoulder pieces fashioned on top. The men walked back and forth in regular order one after the other, four crewmen to the side as they pushed the long boat up stream. There was a windlass on the front with a rope attached. When the boat was brought to the rapids or shoals, it was necessary for one man to take the end of the long rope and wade upstream until he came to a point above the rapids where the rope was tied to a tree. Then was begun the task of turning the windlass so as to pull the boat while some pushed with their spikepoles and others kept the boat in the middle of the channel.

It was customary for the rivermen who owned and managed boats on the stream to pool their efforts in moving rocks, logs and other debris when

the channel became filled in order to keep boat traffic moving up and down the river.

In the lower reaches of the Tug and Leuvisa there was little difficulty in the management of river boats, but as the traffic proceeded upstream where the fall of the river was more pronounced, the channel might become filled with debris and floating timber, particularly after high tides following the rainy season in the spring.

Just before the advent of the railroad, merchandise along the river became profitable; there were stores open at the mouths of the tributaries of the Tug Fork and Leuvisa. "Brought on goods" were boated up stream to the merchants who either had their individual boats or who hired those with a line of boats engaged in freighting. The "old skillet and lid" was supplanted by the little manufactured step stove, the pride of many a young housewife; and there were many other manufactured articles, such as shoes and boots which took the place of the old homemade moccasins and boots of the hillsmen.

There were few ready made articles of wearing apparel shipped into the hills; however, there were considerable yard goods, such as "store jeans," calico and ginghams which took the weary load from the backs of many of the hard working women of the mountains who sheared the wool, spun the cloth and finally hand sewed the garments into clothing for the family.

Chapter Twelve
Christmas Eve Council Of War

Christmas Eve, 1887 — Meeting at the Home of Devil Anse, a group of six men (Capt. Jim Vance, Charlie Mitchell [alias Gillispie], Johnson Hatfield, Cap Hatfield, Tom Mitchell and Ellison Mounts) decide to kidnap Old Ran'l McCoy and put an end to his agitating the feud. Devil Anse, deciding he was too old and against such an attack, turns his leadership over to Jim Vance.

New Year's Eve, 1887 — It is a bitter cold night with snow and ice on the ground when the party of six approach the McCoy cabin. When the McCoys start siring through the door, the group falls back and returns the fire, igniting a bag of flax on the front porch, setting the house afire. Ran'l's lame daughter, Allifair, runs from the house to pour water on the fire and is shot by mistake in the darkness. Her mother, Sarah, coming to her daughter's aid, is wounded and bludgeoned in the head. Calvin McCoy is shot and killed while running from the front of the cabin providing cover so that his father could escape into the woods and darkness. Ran'l finds his way to a neighbor's and returns to find the bodies of his two dead children and seriously wounded wife (whose hair had actually frozen to the ground from the blood from her wound).

Jan. 10, 1888 — Deputy Frank Phillips, Jim McCoy and thirty other men ride into West Virginia in search of the Hatfields who had burned and murdered on New Year's Eve. Jim Vance and Cap Hatfield, deciding to leave the Hatfield fortress, travel up Thacker Creek to visit Vance's home. Vance and Hatfield fire on the column of McCoys as they ride through a pass in the mountains. In the exchange of bullets, Capt. Vance is wounded sending Cap to warn his father. Avenging the murder of their father, Harmon, Bud

McCoy and Lark McCoy put the finishing bullet into Vance. Cap escapes by borrowing a horse from his Uncle Floyd's farm and shoes from his Uncle Valentine.

Jan. 19, 1888 — By this time, Phillips and his posse capture 9 members of the Hatfield group and take them back into Kentucky for prosecution.

Both state governors are alerted and Governor Wilson of West Virginia orders two companies of militia to protect his border. Yellow journalism nationwide flares highly critical of the states' lack of intervention.

Feb. 1, 1888 — Gov. Wilson issues requisition for release of nine Hatfields illegally held by the State of Kentucky.

Feb. 9, 1888 — Gov. Wilson indicts 28 Kentucky men in the death of Bill Dempsey in 1885.

March 1888 — With militia standing on either side of the KY / WV border, the case goes to the Supreme Court of the nation as to whether Kentucky has the right to hold and try men that have been "abducted" from their home state.

April 1888 — Supreme Court decides Kentucky can try the Hatfield Nine.

Oct. 1888 — Pressure at home has gotten so great that Cap and Johnse Hatfield decide to travel westward and are gone for a total of two years. Nancy McCoy Hatfield, instead of joining her husband as planned, returns to her family where she later marries Frank Phillips, the notorious Pike County Deputy.

Cap and Johnse meet in Spokane Washington Territory, after traveling separately for safety. Through 1889, Cap is farming in Oklahoma under an assumed name; he later stops in Gunnison, Colorado, where he passes himself off as a distant relative of a Civil War widow living there.

Johnse, also under an assumed name, works at logging operations near Spokane. Ran'l McCoy, having been alerted to the Hatfields' itinerary by Nancy McCoy Hatfield, finances a posse of detectives who track Johnse to Washington Territory.

42

Chapter Thirteen
Old Blanket Man

In the fall of 1888, Devil Anse received a letter from a sympathizer in Charleston which read as follows:

Dear Friend Anse,

This is to advise you that I have reliable information that a detective from the capitol city of Ohio is about to visit your area. The purpose of his trip is to plan the extradition of certain citizens of your county to Pike County, Kentucky. His name is John T. Morris, and is disguised as a tramp, carrying a roll of blankets.

Be on the lookout for him and I am sure that you will see to it that he is sent out of your locality with no harm to him.

Sincerely,
Chilton

On a Saturday, Oct. 27, 1888, Dow Steele, a cousin of Devil Anse Hatfield, who lived at the three forks of the creek not far from Horse Pen Mountain, had given out the word far and near to come to his "Corn Shuckin." This affair might have been called a "huskin' bee" in more polite terms in other parts of the country, but these rough and ready mountain folk would not have known a huskin' bee from some stinging insect. It was just a plain, old fashioned corn shuckin' with plenty to eat, including good corn bread, bear meat, and ox-roast.

Here it should be mentioned that vigilance was a watchword not merely in the household of the Hatfields, but with their loyal friends who lived near the mountain gaps, the creek forks and the highways where any suspicious looking traveler would be watched with curious anxiety. Cap, one of Anse' nine boys, was stationed at the old log school house down the main road upon which "the old blanket man" was expected. Cap looked down the rocky way and saw what appeared to be an elderly man hobbling along toward him carrying a roll of what might have been bed blankets sheathed in a waterproof covering. His hair and beard were long and he had a hole in his peak-topped hat through which a strand of hair protruded. His suit was old and ragged at the elbows, patches on the knees and frayed at the bottom of the trousers. Cap stepped from behind a big birch tree near the log school house with his new '73 Winchester in hand. He hollered, "How's the old blanket man this morning?" The stranger tried to assume surprise and astonishment at such an abrupt salutation from a young armed mountaineer whom he had never seen before. "You're alookin' for my old pappy, the one they call Devil Anse, ain't ye?"

"Why, no, young man, I'm an old man traveling across the country on my way south before the winter begins."

"Well, I'll go up the road with ye a mile or so," said Cappy. "They've got a big corn shuckin' and plenty to eat and drink up at the three forks where everybody is gatherin' in.

I knowed you were the old blanket man when I saw them on your back."

"Where do you see any blankets?" inquired the traveler.

"I don't see any blankets exactly, anymore than you can see the bullet in the bottom of this rifle, but I know the blankets are there."

"I'm sure we'll have no treble," said the old man.

"Oh, I'm not looking for any trouble myself," said Cap, "but I don't know what's going to happen to you when you get up to the corn shuckin'."

As they walked up the rocky trail the young mountaineer kept his guest in front of him as the elder one glanced back suspiciously at the long barrel of the gun to see which way it was pointing.

"Don't be afraid of this gun; we never sneak up on anybody like a detective or shoot them in the back," said Cap.

Soon they were at the three forks where the main creek had the left fork on the one side and right fork on the other. Dow Steele's log house stood there in the opening with the log barn, cowl crib and other buildings farther in the distance. It was obvious from the number of horses there were plenty of corn shuckers on hand. A large log fire was burning where preparations were being made for an ox roast.

Cap announced their arrival; out came Devil Anse with a 45-90 Winchester in hand and motioned for them to gather round. A hickory bottomed rocking chair was brought out in the open and the old blanket man was invited to sit down.

Cap acted as interrogator: "So you are the blanket man; we've been hearing about you long before you got here. We understand you have been camping along the road since you struck the water sheds of this valley and that you've been having it a little hard living on chestnuts and black walnuts and maybe a few apples along the road. What is your real name, Mr. Blanket Man? "

The guest, trying to pretend a lack of comprehension and to assume an air of drollery, gave short answers in disjointed sentences. "I'm Jerimiah Seece, traveling through the country. I have no home of my own; I'm going to North Carolina where my grandpa was raised."

"Where did you come from lately," asked Cap.

"I come from Big Take, up North. Crossed big river and walked many miles. I sleep out under trees in a blanket bed. I no like stay in people's houses. I have catching ailment."

"If you stay out all the time, why are your hands so white and clean on the back and just walnut stains on your palms?"

"I have to eat nuts."

"Would you mind pulling off your shoes? If you have walked for many months, why are the blisters on your feet like a man not used to walking?"

"Well," said Cap. "Come out behind the barn and corn crib. Come along all you boys, I want you to look Jerimiah over so you will know him the next time you see him, provided we don't bed him down up in the timber with a nice blanket of leaves."

The blanket man was "invited" to pull off his ragged coat, shirt and trousers; underneath was a brand new suit of clothes that still smelled of moth balls. Also among his things, Cap found a 138 Smith & Wesson breakdown, a box of shells with seal unbroken, a few cans of corned beef and $66 in currency.

"Let's hurry along," said Cap. "You're not Jerimiah Seece, you are John T. Morris, a mail order detective from Columbus, Ohio. We know all about you; we heard you were coming along before you got here. You ain't fooling nobody. We know your history. You had better operate where you can get your bearings. You're clear out of your latitude up here in these hills and hollers. You're plumb lost. Now, Mr. City Slicker, we're not going to leave you up in the woods or hang you to an apple tree and shoot your hide full of holes, but we're giving you back your gun, ammunition and your greenbacks and you may need your blankets, too. One thing's for sure: don't let the sun go down on you in the watersheds of this valley. You go back the way you come and you will find one of our neighbors down the creek about four miles who will have his boy take you on horseback till you reach the county line. So git goin', Mr. Blanket Man."

Chapter Fourteen
Johnse, Far From Kentucky

During the fall of 1888, while looking about Spokane, Washington,
Johnse said that he felt secure being
far from Kentucky where he thought
that few, if any, had ever heard of the
Hatfield and McCoy feud, but just
then he looked across the street and
saw a saloon. In the window a sign
said, "Fine Kentucky Whiskey,"
whereupon he decided that if Kentucky Whiskey was reaching as far
as Spokane, he had better move on.
He soon took a job from a timber
company up the river, working in
the big trees.

Previous to leaving for the Northwest, the matter was discussed
among the Hatfields for several weeks, long before there was any anticipa-
tion that Nancy would take her children and go back to her people. Johnse
had confided all of this to Nancy and promised that when he became settled
in Washington Territory that he would send for her and Anse and Stella,
their two little ones. However, the blood of family kindred and feeling for
her kinspeople ran deeper than any marriage relationship between members of the warring factions. So Nancy confided to her family that Johnse
would likely be headed for the Far West.

Acting upon this clue, Old Dan, Alf Burnett, Treve Brown, Kentucky

Bill and three other detectives set out for Washington Territory in search of Johnse Hatfield. Expenses for the men were paid by Randall McCoy.

They eventually went to a timbering camp on the Snoqualmie River and inquired at the headquarters, giving the description of young Hatfield. They were told that there was a young blue-eyed, light-haired, West Virginian there who said his name was Jim Jacobs. While the detectives were making their preliminary investigation, a young woman who had become acquainted with Jacobs wrote a note and sent it by a half-breed Indian named Joe Speed Siwash. The note, written to the foreman of the logging crew, simply said, "Tell Jim to look out." It was signed, "Midgie Staunton McCarthy." As they looked down the valley they saw seven men coming, and Johnse threw down his ax just in time to escape into the timberland, as the foreman directed the Indian to help him find his way across the river. He concealed himself in a thicket and watched his pursuers searching the rocks and caverns in the mountains. Later Johnse remarked: "I never spent such terrible hours as I did watching them hunt for me. A big flock of Canadian jaybirds, which the Indian called whiskey dicks, surrounded the thicket where I was hidden and kept up such a chatter that anybody that was acquainted with such critters would have known that they were all het up about something, but them detectives never suspicioned the birds and went on around and searched everywhere but the place where I was hidden. Just as soon as I got a break and the coast was clear, I swam across the river. It was the only way out. I went to Seattle and caught a steamer to British Columbia and got a job cuttin' trees for two years. Them trees were so big that you had to scaffold up above the roots and drive a slab in the side to stand on, in order to get close enough to chop it down."

The search was so persistent in Washington Territory that Vinson, a feuding friend to Devil Anse living in Spokane, contacted Johnse and obtained a lock of his hair; then a letter was written to Johnse' mother, stating that her son had been killed in an accident while felling trees. For a period of two years the Hatfields believed him dead, but on one clear autumn evening late in the fall of 1890, a well-dressed stranger dismounted at Devil Anse' gate, and before Mother Louvicey knew what was happening, she was grasped in the arm of her wayward boy, home at last from the Far Northwest.

Chapter Fifteen
1890: Industrialization Opens The Mountains

Cap and Johnse return to West Virginia by late 1889. Johnse married Rebecca Browning, and the newlyweds receive 300 acres of timberland from her father. Cap turns to farming.

New governors for both West Virginia and Kentucky are sympathetic to appeals on both sides.

The trial of the nine members of the Hatfield gang had just concluded. Ran'l McCoy was never satisfied that Devil Anse, Cap, Johnse and others were still at large and unpunished.

1891-92 — Bounty hunters and detectives still prowl the hills. Yellow journalism continues to attribute mountain deaths to the Hatfield-McCoy feud, and in truth it will never be known how many actually died because of this particular family battle. Cap Hatfield announces through the local newspaper that a general amnesty has been agreed on and a wedding between a Hatfield and a McCoy is announced.

1893 — Colonel Buffalo Bill Cody comes to eastern Kentucky with his Wild West show. It's said that Devil Anse steps out from the audience and matches shots with the famous Indian fighter and buffalo hunter. As the audience cheers, the Hatfield patriarch proves again his perfect aim.

But the true changes that came to the mountain areas greatly influenced the lives of isolated mountain communities and sought to develop the wealth of natural resources there. Not long before the end of the nineteenth century, industrialists from metropolitan areas focused their attention on the Allegheny Mountains near the border lines of the Virginias and Kentucky. What was once the rough and rugged hunting grounds of the Indians now became the dream of those looking toward the beds of coal, oil and gas which lay beneath, to say nothing of the virgin timber which covered the mountains and valleys. The first railroad came down the New River, opening up one of the greatest coal producing regions on the continent. Prospectors came riding up and down in all directions seeking to purchase lands, minerals and timber. The development that followed rivaled the Gold Rush history of the Rocky Mountains and, for the most part, has been more far reaching in its continued development and impact upon the economy of the nation.

A new day now appeared to be dawning: news of industrial activity and large surveying crews were coming in from the East; the supplies were being brought to them by push-blats from the West. Previous anxiety over advancing feud raiders was now changed to a different sort of excitement: a railroad was to be built along the dividing line of the two states. Next came industrial representatives bargaining for rights-of-way — the location of depots and railroad yards. Then came thousands of workers; shantytowns went up. Brown men from the South, hitherto strangers to the hill people, brought about a mighty change in the interest of the mountain folk from feuding and fussing to working and worshiping along the border.

1895 — Devil Anse Hatfield operates a timber and saw mill operation, and acquires quite a bit of wealth from the sale of land to railroad and coal interests.

Rebecca Browning Hatfield dies, leaving Johnse with three babies. Johnse goes to work on the railroad line.

1896 — Ran'l McCoy operates a ferryboat (as he had done for years), still ranting to his passengers about the burning of his home almost a decade ago.

November 1896 — Cap Hatfield and his step-son, Joe Glenn, Jr., go to Thacker to celebrate the Presidential Election.

1897 — Cap and Joe Glenn, his stepson, are involved in a shoot out where three are killed. They are captured, tried and sentenced: Cap to one year, Joe Glenn to reform school.

Cap escapes jail two weeks before his release date; prior to this he had proven himself a model prisoner. He had come to learn of a kidnapping attempt that was to have been made upon his release. Randall McCoy shows up to join the posse sent out to recapture Cap; however, Cab eludes them.

In 1898, while working on the railroad on the West Virginia/Kentucky line, Johnse Hatfield is kidnapped by six men and taken to Pike County to face charges dating back to the burning of the McCoy home, New Year's Eve, 1887. The kidnapping was planned by a rival and financed by Doc Ellis, a man who had attended Cap Hatfield's trial two years before and had taken a disliking to the family. Johnse is tried and sentenced to life.

July 1899 — Elias Hatfield, younger brother to Johnse, "happened" to come upon Doc Ellis in Williamson and challenges him to a duel. Ellis is killed and Elias is tried for premeditation. Elias is defended by former Governor Wilson and is sentenced to life.

1900 — Elias Hatfield is pardoned.

Chapter Sixteen
Turn Of The Century

By 1900, Anerson "Devil Anse" Hatfield is living as a well-to-do gentleman farmer; he owns a logging operation and sawmill.

Ran'l McCoy continues to operate a ferry, still complaining to passengers of the 1888 attack on his home.

Cap Hatfield's wife teaches her husband to read and write. This opens up a whole new world to the feudist; he goes on to study law and eventually sets up practice in the City of Logan.

1903 — Elias and Troy Hatfield ride the railroad line as detectives, to protect passengers and crew from "bushwhack" and robbery.

In 1904, Elias Hatfield's repeated appeals to the Kentucky Governor to pardon Johnse Hatfield are ignored in spite of the warden's recommendation. Johnse had saved his life during a prison riot. The Lieutenant Governor finally pardons Johnse while the governor is out of state.

Devil Anse Hatfield testifies at the trial of the peddler murderer.

In 1910, Elias and Troy open a saloon in Booner. An Italian liquor peddler infringes on their territory and when challenged by the Hatfields, all three die in a shoot-out. Devil Anse, 71, is devastated by the death of his sons.

1911 — A circuit-ridin' minister, Uncle Dyke Garrett, who had earlier become a close friend to the Hatfield patriarch, consoles him in his grief and Devil Anse eventually decides to be baptized. The ceremony took place on Main Island Creek. It is believed that Cap and Johnse were also baptized that day with their father.

Historian Robert Y. Spence once wrote the following concerning Dyke Garrett and the Hatfield baptism: "Uncle Dyke Garrett was very proud of two achievements in his long life. One was the baptism of J. Green Mc-

Neely. The other was the baptism of Anderson (Devil Anse) Hatfield. The baptism of McNeely gave him much help with his ministry because McNeely also became a preacher. The two traveled together through the county until the end of Garrett's life.

"The second baptism is probably Garrett's most well remembered action. Hatfield, whose family was involved in the bitter feud that tore through Logan County and Pike County, Kentucky, in the 1880s and 1890s, was baptized in Island Creek in October 1911. Garrett, who always had called his friend by his proper name, Anderson, instead of the more popular nickname, Devil Anse, remembered that day with more happiness than any other, according to some of Garrett's closest friends.

"When the ceremony ended, he mounted his horse and rode to Crooked Creek, where he often shared a meal with the family of Scott McDonald. That day, after he said grace, he turned to young Mollie McDonald and smiled. 'Well, Mollie,' he said grinning. 'I baptized the devil today.' Perhaps that baptism gave Garrett so much joy because he and Hatfield had been fellow members of Camp Straton United Confederate Veterans."

According to Spence, Dr. Sidney B. Lawson, a physician in the City of Logan in the late nineteenth and early twentieth century, once documented life in Logan County at the turn of the century, and told of a specific event at a local banking institution: "Conditions and people in all walks of life have changed in the last half a century. Personal relationships and social and friendly intercourse are not now anything like they used to be. No one has the time, in their frenzied efforts to make a living for themselves and their families in the modern whirl, to care much or consider very deeply how others live.

"Yet there were still many minutes in Logan when that wasn't strictly true. By the end of the 1910s the Logan National Bank had become settled in place, while the violence of the Hatfield-McCoy feud already had become a distant memory.

"'One day I was working in the Logan National Bank,' Merrill Atkinson once told Dr. Lawson, 'when Cap and Devil Anse Hatfield came in with their rifles. They wanted some records of a few deposits that Devil Anse had made for evidence in a lawsuit he was in.

"'He had made the deposits two or three years before then and, since the files were buried down in the basement, it took two or three days to dig them out.

"'They told me to go down and hunt for them because Devil Anse needed them that week. As I remember it, he came in on a Saturday morning and I had to have the records the next Saturday.

"'When he came back the next week to pick them up,' Atkinson added, 'he and Cap had a big basket with them. In it he had a jug of some extra fine moonshine for Naaman Jackson and (George W.) Raike, who was the bookkeeper there.

"'Now he didn't want to leave me out. Devil Anse was a very thoughtful man. But because I was just a kid, he couldn't give me any whiskey. So he gave me a jug just like the others, but was full of honey. He said, 'Here, son. You did all the work on this, and these other fellows didn't do any of it.'"

Later in 1911, Johnse marries Lettie Toler and they have a son, Luther.

1912 — Henry D. Hatfield becomes Republican governor of West Virginia; one of his strongest supporters happens to be a McCoy.

1914 — Ran'l McCoy dies of burns suffered from a fall into an open fire. The McCoy family grieves over their proud, strong patriarch. According to reports, he died "full of bitterness."

1921 — Devil Anse Hatfield dies of natural causes. He was 83 and reportedly "had a clear and forgiving conscience." His obituary appears in the *New York Times*.

Locally, in the *Williamson Daily News*, the newspaper in Mingo County, the death notice headline stated: "Devil Anse Is No More; Checks Out With Boots Off At Hospitable Mountain Home. Dauntless Spirit of Feud Leader Feared By Foes But Esteemed and Admired By Friends Is Translated From Mountains He Loved So Well to the Realms of the Great Unknown."

Throngs of people who came by foot, mule or a special section of the railroad, attended Devil Anse' funeral. During the solemn event, the McCoys and Hatfields stand together in the pouring rain. Uncle Dyke conducted the funeral and Hatfield's body was incased in a $2,000 casket and laid to rest in a steel vault built some years earlier on Hatfield's farm.

Obituary Of
Devil Anse Hatfield

The *Bluefield Daily Telegraph and
Williamson Daily News, January 8, 1921*, read:

WILLIAMSON, W.Va., Jan. 7, 1921 — Reports reaching Williamson tonight were that Devil Anse Hatfield, leader of the clan in the Hatfield-McCoy feud in the 80's and 90's, had died at his home on Island Creek, Logan county, of pneumonia last night. Relatives here were without word of the death.

Anderson ("Devil Anse") Hatfield was one of the leaders of the historic feud between the Hatfield and McCoy families in the mountains of West Virginia and northern Kentucky. Shot at from ambush and in hand-to-hand combat scores of times with the McCoys, he had always predicted he would live to die a natural death, as he now has at the age of eighty, without bearing any marks of battle.

"Devil Anse" had a reputation as a crack shot, that was known throughout the mountainous region of the two states, and at the age of seventy he could shoot a squirrel out of the tallest timber. He often turned the trick for admirers, with the old rifle that he carried ready for action at all hours, and with which during the early eighties, he would shoot on sight any member of the McCoy family.

The celebrated feud of the Hatfield family with the McCoys was started over some hogs, one of the Hatfields winning a lawsuit that was brought to determine their ownership. Soon after that a brother of "Devil Anse" was shot and wounded in more than fifteen places by one of the McCoys. The feud then started and did not end until the few remaining McCoys went over into Kentucky, where they now reside.

"Devil Anse" had none of the attributes of the "bad men" in his character. He always was recognized as a loyal friend of the many with whom he was acquainted. Numbered among those who believed he had been right in the position he took during the feud days, were the late Judge John J. Jackson, known as the "Iron Judge," who was appointed to the federal bench by President Lincoln, and former Governor E. W. Wilson, the former protecting Hatfield form [sic] capture when he had been called into court, and the latter refusing to honor a requisition of the governor of Kentucky, for the arrest of "Devil Anse" on a charge of killing some particular member of the McCoy family. Detectives, real and alleged, had arranged for the capture of Hatfield, spurred by a reward, after they had seen to it that he was indicted on a charge of whiskey selling, in 1888. Judge Jackson was on the bench at the time and was informed of the danger that awaited the accused man. Judge Jackson sent word to Hatfield that if he would appear in court with out an officer being sent for him, the court would see that he had ample protection until he returned to his home in Logan County.

Hatfield appeared and was acquitted of the charge against him. Some of the detectives pounced upon him soon after he left the court room, but Judge Jackson summoned all of them before him, and threatened to send them all to jail, directing special officers to see that Hatfield was permitted to reach his home. After Hatfield was well on his way, Judge Jackson told the detectives that if they wanted their man they would have to get him, just like the Mc-Coys had been trying to do for a number of years. They never went.

"Anse" Hatfield spent the last fifteen years of his life quietly and peaceably on a small farm he owned in Logan County. He raised a good many hogs and but seldom left his community. Once he was prevailed upon by some enterprising amusement manager to go on the vaudeville stage. He made all preparations to do so but abandoned the idea when an old indictment was produced, which had been quashed on condition that the old mountaineer agree to remain at home the rest of his days.

Hatfield was born in Logan County, West Virginia, but then in the domain of the Old Dominion, in 1841, a short distance from the old cabin in which he died.

1921 — Before long, a $3,000 marble likeness of the feud leader is erected over his grave at the family plot at Sarah Ann, in Logan County.

1928 — Tennis Hatfield shakes hands with Uncle Jim McCoy and "officially ends the feud."

1929 — The wife of Devil Anse Hatfield, Louvicey Chafin Hatfield, dies.

1930 — Cap Hatfield dies of brain tumor.

1938 — Uncle Dyke Garrett dies, at the age of 96.

May 22, 1944 — *Life Magazine* runs a feature on the feuding clans, entitled, "Life Visits the Hatfields and McCoys: famous feuding families now live together in peace," which includes a variety of photographs and interview material from living family members. By this time the feud has taken on mythical proportions, and the facts surrounding the often bloody family quarrel were mostly clouded in misinformation, falsehoods or in a grandiose stretching of the truth.

An excerpt from the article:

"The Hatfield-McCoy feud is celebrated in song and legend, but surprisingly few authentic facts have been written about it. The surviving Hatfields and McCoys are close-mouthed folk who do not kill each other any more, but dislike talking to strangers."

The national magazine feature included black and white photographs of white-bearded Hark Hatfield, 73, and his wife, Ollie "McCoy" Hatfield, and a photograph of the Hatfield cemetery and Devil Anse statue, in Sarah Ann, WV. Other photographs in the 10-cent issue included Bud and Rhoda McCoy, Joe D. Hatfield (holding the shirt worn by his uncle Ellison on the day he was killed by three McCoys) and L. Lawson Hatfield. There were also shots including the flat bridge reaching over to the Devil Anse Hatfield homeplace (the property once had a makeshift draw-bridge for security reasons), the Cal McCoy headstone and Bud McCoy family cottage.

Chapter Seventeen

Four Deer With One Bullet

The following story was remembered and documented by Coleman A. Hatfield as one of the tales Anderson "Devil Anse" Hatfield told to his grandchildren. It was later told to Coleman C. Hatfield by his father, as well.

"Now," said Devil Anse Hatfield to his grandchildren, "I'll never forget the time when I brought home four deer with one shot. I know that most folk won't believe what I say, but it's true. We were huntin' in the mountains where there was a long logging road where timber had been hauled down the slope, and I was at the upper end watching for deer to cross. My brother had gone around the ridge to get in behind the deer where they were feeding, and he was told to turn the dogs loose and 'halloo' them back in my direction, so I took a stand and was watchin'.

"I heard the dogs yelping, coming nearer and nearer down the ridge and headed for a long hollow where they would cross. It wasn't long till I saw an old doe and a half grown buck trot up into the 'haul' road about a hundred yards down the slope; when they got into the open they squatted to the ground resting and I fired, and the bullet passed through both their bodies. I hurried down to bleed them as we always do, and then I gutted them to take out the entrails and — believe it or not — two fawns, which were ready to be born, raised up, and there I had the little ones to take home to be raised on the bottle.

"So, with one bullet I brought home four deer."

Chapter Eighteen
The Federal Court Story

August 1889 — The Hatfield Nine are tried and sentenced: Ellison Mounts turns state's evidence, confesses to the murder of Allifair McCoy and is the only one sentenced to hang. Valentine Hatfield, certain he will be exonerated, is imprisoned for life and dies in prison one year later.

September 1889 — The hills of both states crawl with bounty hunters. Participants are constantly on the alert and establish a mountain warning system...many innocent mountain people and strangers are killed trying to win the large bounties; many "disappearances" and deaths by bushwhackers are attributed to this feud. It was even rumored that Frank James, the infamous bank robber, was confronted by Devil Anse on one mountain pass and asked to find some other part of the mountain region to pass through.

November 1889 — Devil Anse Hatfield appears in Charleston, West Virginia, to answer fabricated charges of selling whiskey without a license.

Dave Stratton, a West Virginia native, had marital ties in Kentucky where he often visited his wife's people and came in contact with McCoy sympathizers. He was looked upon by the Hatfields as one to be watched even though his father, Major Stratton, had served in the war with Devil Anse. The two families and their near relatives were friendly except that Dave was regarded by some as being tricky, which proved later at the battle of Grapevine Creek where he was in the lead guiding the McCoys into the Hatfield territory.

Previous to that time he had visited the home of Devil Anse on Tug Fork under the pretext of selling Anse some merchandise that had been brought up on a pushboat from down the river. Among other things, Anse bought six bridles and saddles. In exchange Dave took some calves which were loaded on the boat on the return trip to the market down below. During the transaction, Anse had given Dave a drink of brandy from a gallon jug. After the trade was over Dave insisted on buying what remained of the brandy, but Anse said he wouldn't sell it ... he would *give* it to him.

This incident was related to Dan Cunningham and other detectives who insisted that Dave Stratton make a trip to Charleston to appear before the next Federal Grand jury and indict Anderson Hatfield for selling liquor without a license. The whole scheme was to get Anse over to the state capital, where he would be helpless and away from his area of defenses. The detectives were jubilant that they were about to cash in on the rewards that were offered for delivery of Devil Anse and others to Kentucky.

After the indictment was returned, Bill White, United States Marshall, was dispatched from the Federal Court on an 85 mile trip to the home of Hatfield on Island Creek. Up to this time none of the family knew of the indictment which had been returned upon the information furnished by Dave Stratton.

There was no road south of the Great Kanawha River and practically all travel was on horseback. Very few roads were sufficiently passable to permit wagon or buggy travel. On one November morning in '89, a U.S. Marshall riding a black horse was headed southward, armed with a warrant from Federal Judge Jonathan M. Jackson seeking to apprehend Devil Anse Hatfield and bring him to the U.S. District Court. Within the last few miles of the Hatfield stronghold, all the neighbors and friends of the Hatfields looked wide-eyed as the officer queried them regarding the distance and the exact location of the Hatfield home. These concerned friends knew that this fast horse carrying the Marshall would reach Devil Anse before their warning could.

Just before the Marshall reached Devil Anse' gate, he was met by more than a half dozen barking, growling bear dogs with their bristles standing up as they crowded in the way of the approaching rider. A young woman appeared at the gate in front of the house, hushed the dogs and asked the stranger what his business was. Feigning caution for his safety, she asked him not to dismount until she returned, or the dogs might bite him. She rushed into the house and soon there appeared on his front porch, brown-bearded Devil Anse Hatfield with his long hair curling upward near his shoulders. He was dressed in a hunting shirt, homemade breeches and high-topped, slip-on boots. They exchanged greetings, and the officer told Devil Anse the nature of his business. He was then offered dinner and was ushered into the old mountaineer's home where he laid aside his hat. He and his host made preparation to sit down to the table which was spread before them.

During the meal, Devil Anse explained what had actually happened with the brandy and gave his word that he would appear for trial in Charleston in three weeks. The Marshall accepted Devil Anse' word, for he had heard a great deal about this man. The officer mounted his horse and rode away believing as he went that Anse' word was as good as his bond. After the officer's return to the capitol, he assured the Court that the accused would be there on the trial day.

For the next three weeks the Hatfield camp was busy making preparations for Devil Anse to make the journey across the mountains to the capital city in the Kanawha Valley. The sentinels were out and the neighbors were watching the gaps and passes of the hills where the roads led from Kentucky, but there was no danger of any raid, at least for the present, since the detectives who were working along the border were keeping quiet and planning how they would trap Devil Anse when he reached the capital city. Many old friends, such as Uncle Harve Duty, came and offered friendly advice. He felt Anse was riding into a trap but he was reassured by Devil Anse that nonetheless, he was a man of his word at all times and thus, he fully intended to travel with a company of his men.

In the meantime everybody who was to join in the trip was shining his boots and rubbing them with groundhog grease to make them walk easy. All the good wearin' clothes and hats were being brushed with the old turkey wing brush and all the shirts were being washed and repaired for the boys to make the trip. Many of the younger lads speculated as to what the trip might mean and looked forward to it with considerable enjoyment.

Devil Anse, with seventeen followers, all armed except himself, set out on the march across the mountains toward the West Virginia capital. Their course took them down Turtle Creek and Spruce River, across Big Coal and over Drawdy Mountain. It was late fall, and they cooked and camped by the fires where they rested at night. In those days most of the roads, particularly through the gaps, were no more than bridle paths and the country was heavily timbered.

They shot squirrels and pheasants as they went along and broiled their game whenever they were hungry. Early the morning of the fourth day they appeared out of the woods on the south bank of the Kanawha River opposite Charleston, where the ferry would take them across the river.

Immediately curious crowds began to gather on the other side of the Great Kanawha wondering who the bewhiskered, long-haired, slouch-hatted mountaineer was leading this retinue of armed followers, made up of both old and young, oddly dressed in their backwoods garb, all carrying a non-descript variety of cap-lock squirrel rifles, mussel loading shotguns, shot pouches, powder horns, haversacks loaded with ammunition and a few new '73 Winchester repeating rifles.

Down at the mouth of Ferry Branch they were picked up and taken to the north side of the river, where the crowd began to back off and separate as the visitors marched up the riverbank on the way to the Federal Courthouse. Devil Anse first inquired about U.S. Marshall Bill White. When they reached the place, attaches ushered them into waiting rooms to rest before the opening of the Court. They had plenty of time to relax, and it was after a while that the Marshall, hearing that Devil Anse had arrived, came hurrying in to greet his prisoner and to thank the old mountaineer for living up to his promise. The officer expressed surprise at so many armed followers and Anse replied that he needed every one to bring him in as promised.

The Marshall explained that it would be more than an hour before court opened and that they could place their guns in the corner and go upstairs and sit in the courtroom, but they all said that they wished to hold onto their "weepins." As soon as the Judge appeared on the bench and all of the preliminaries were completed, Devil Anse' bodyguards filed into the courtroom and took their seats, resting their guns between their knees as they watched Devil Anse march up with the U.S. Marshall to the bar of the court. By this time, the courtroom was crowded with spectators, filling all the seats in the room. After attorneys sitting at the counsel tables made a few motions, His Honor, Judge Jonathan M. Jackson, called to the clerk to announce the first case on the docket.

The clerk called out in a loud tone: "First case, United States vs. Anderson Hatfield," whereupon the Court called upon the accused to enter his plea of guilty or not guilty. "Judge, Your Honor, I ain't guilty. You see, it was this way..."

So Devil Anse, in his own mountain vernacular, proceeded to tell the court how Dave Stratton and his gang of detectives had been trying to trap him for years. He then told the Court of the truth behind the "whiskey sale."

The District Attorney arose and addressed the Court, saying that following an investigation, he believed Devil Anse not guilty of the charges. And in addition he also believed there was a plot afoot to get Hatfield away from his home.

The venerable jurist rapped for order and said that he was dropping the charges, and he charged the U.S. Marshall to protect Devil Anse on his trip home to Logan County. Devil Anse rose and addressed the Court. He thanked the Judge and stated that he was indeed most anxious to be gettin' home. Before court was dismissed, the Judge, being the sort of individual that he was known to be, spoke to the Marshall and told him to bring Mr. Hatfield back into his chambers where he could speak with him.

The Marshall escorted the old feud leader with a few from his company back into the Judge's private offices, and here was enacted one of the friendliest visits that the old feudist had ever enjoyed. His Honor seemed to forget for the moment that he was a Judge of the U.S. Court and dropped all formality, talking at length with Devil Anse about bear hunting, raccoons and wild hogs and what-have-you. The Judge then asked to see Anse' gun, and Anse unbuttoned his hunting jacket and reached way down and drew out a bright new six-inch barreled, breakdown 44 Smith & Wesson. In turn, Devil Anse invited the Judge into the hills to go bear hunting. Then the Marshall called several of his aides, who took Devil Anse and his men to the ferryboat which they were to ride across the river. By this time the whole city was in excitement over the visitors who had come to town. There must have been a few thousand on the bank as the ferry boat pulled away across the river. They waved to the old mountaineer as he stood on the end of the boat waving back with his red bandana; before they were out of sight, the men and boys on the bank shouted as they threw their hats in the air, "Goodbye, Devil Anse! Come back and see us again!"

Chapter Nineteen
Rafting The Leatherwood Shoals Of The Guyan

The logging crews and their hearty ox teams had been busy in the timberland above the "roughs" of the Guyan during the late, dry summer and early fall. The stroke of the woodcutters' axes and falling of timber resounded in the hills and hollows along the shoals. Great care had been taken in seasoning the sharp hickory pins to be driven through the augur holes in the seasoned oak ties that bound the big logs together. Every raft was equipped with a thirty foot, hickory or white oak pole mounted upon the top of a cost near the rear end of the raft, which allowed the free swinging of the oar.

At the end of the pole in the center back, submerged in the water, was a twelve-foot blade making the overall length of pole and oar approximately forty feet. Two fifteen-foot oars were mounted on the right front and another on the left front, all of which perfected the mobility of the raft. As good fortune would have it, the heavy fall rains began and the river commenced to rise as the rafts creaked and tugged at the heavy cables, which secured them to the trees on the bank. All hands had gathered and old Preachin' Ellis Toler, known for his loud voice, was bossing the preparation of the departure of the fleet of timber rafts to be guided on the twenty-five mile trip from Clear Fork down through dangerous Leatherwood Shoals to Gilbert and on down the turbulent Guyan.

The old bearded timberchief mounted the foremost raft to pilot those that followed down the winding gorge. Red Morgan was at the right bow of the foremost raft and Skid Browning at the left. Tom Wallace and Cap Hatfield were operating the big oar that steered the raft, with the great blade reaching into the river behind. Cap had secured his rifle to the upper end of the lar and tied his bear dog to the lower end just above the water. Old shaggy-browed Toler stood erect, looking downstream as he bellowed from the bull's horn which he held to his mouth. The big cable was untied from the tree and wound up and fastened on the rear of the raft, and they were off.

"Every man to his oar: bow to the left," boomed the voice of the old timberchief from the bull's horn, as the great raft rushed creaking down the first fall of the gorge. The water swirled up around the knees of the oarsmen. The bear dog howled, scrambling and swimming as the muddy water dashed over the logs. The old bull's horn sounded off, "Red Morgan, bow to the right. Bow to the right!" as they approached the tall steep cliffs, which rose two hundred feet on either side above the dashing waters of the river that roared along the base of the high cliffs.

All the other crews were manning their rafts and joining in the race as they strung out one after the other, spaced at a safe distance so as to avoid overtaking the crew ahead. Veteran timbercutter, Johnse Hatfield, was the captain of the next raft, following Bull Horn Toler. At the call of the leader of each crew, the oarsmen leaned hard to follow the command to swing from side to side, pulling hard to avoid the boulders and cliffs which must be shunned — where a single mistake might dash the logs asunder, with the very real chance that all might be drowned.

During the years of timbering on this rushing river such disasters had occurred: many rafts were torn apart, and the crews either drowned or miraculously escaped by riding the logs on to safety.

The timber crews rode their great logs through the falling Guyan waters until they guided out into the smoother river toward the Ohio country, where their merchandise was anchored near the big towns and sold to be manufactured into lumber.

At first the demand was for the black walnut logs and later for the mighty poplar and red oaks. When the tides had subsided and the rafts were sold, the men from the hills came back up the Ohio as far as steamboat traffic would bring them, and there they obtained supplies to be loaded on push-boats and sent upstream.

This was the commercial life of the hillmen in the 1880s and early '90s, as they floated their wares down to market and exchanged them for the factory goods that were "brought on from below."

Chapter Twenty
Riverboat Battles

It had been a busy week in the Kentucky river town of Catlettsburg, where the Ohio met the Big Sandy. The timbermen from Leuvisa and Tug Fork were selling their rafts to the dealers. For a mile or more back up the Sandy, great rafts of walnut, oak and poplar had been tied to the trees along the banks. It was Saturday and the logging boys were whooping it up in the saloons on Main Street. Everybody had been paid, and they were getting ready to celebrate the return trip up the Sandy as far as the steamboats would take them.

All were planning to board the boats on their last run up the river in the evening. The Bromleys controlled the *Fleetwing* boats, and Captain Michael Friese was owner of a rival line that included the *Mountain Boy*, the *Mountain Girl* and the *Fanny Friese*. All of the surplus cartridges had been bought up in town, including supplies of gunpowder, bar lead and a few bullet molds, to say nothing of bright new H&H break-down Smith & Wessons and Colt pistols. It was noticed that the raftsmen from the Leuvisa Fork were celebrating in the old John Watson Saloon down at the corner, while the Tug Forkers were whooping it up in Major Vincent's Bar further up the street. Chief of Police Chuck Richardson had deployed his men in the middle ground, keeping the rival factions from mingling, at least while they were in town. Late in the afternoon the old *Fleetwing* was heard coming up the river, sounding its low lonesome signal for the landing. Then it was then that everybody in Watson's Saloon headed for the landing, where the sidewheeler was bound up the Sandy. The passengers, made up entirely of Kentucky boys in their homemade boots and jeans, hunting shirts and slouch hats, were well-armed, with plenty of ammunition and "likker" to keep 'em happy. They were hardly aboard when the shrill sounds of the *Mountain Boy* were heard blowing for Friese Landing, where the bearded captain would take his cargo headed for the Tug Fork of Sandy.

The *Fleetwing* swung off the landing and maneuvered toward midstream, passing the *Mountain Boy* just as the latter was preparing to move off shore. There were no women or children on the passenger list of either boat; the men from both vessels peered at each other while the *Fleetwing* pulled ahead.

"There's Big Jim McCoy on the *Fleetwing*," shouted one of the Hatfields who stood among other Tug Forkers on the deck of the *Mountain Boy*.

"Let's give 'em a race, Captain Friese," shouted a dozen voices.

"All right boys," said the Captain, "We'll do just that."

As soon as the rear vessel could get under way, the old steamboat captain gave orders to fire the boiler, throw on the fuel, and full steam ahead, and then the *Mountain Boy* started after the *Fleetwing* which had now gotten well ahead up the river.

It was apparent that the Leuvisa rivermen had conveniently boarded the front vessel while the Tugites had boarded the other, and the race was on. The crowd stood on the rear of the forward boat, yelling and taunting the others who had now gathered on the front deck of the *Mountain Boy*, following in hot pursuit.

The range of pistol shot was a little too great; nevertheless, the crowds on both boats began loading and firing their new 38s, 41s and 44 Colts and Smith & Wessons, with the shots falling short of the distance that separated the steaming, roaring boats as their big wheels churned and slashed the muddy waters of Sandy, while each fought the breast of the stream.

"Pitch in," ordered the Captain. "Some of you boys help fire the boilers, soak that firewood with lamp oil and feed it as fast as it will take it!"

Major Bromley was waving and gesticulating at Captain Friese, who returned the waving in a manner which puzzled the passengers.

"I'd like to see 'em get together and fist it out with each other," roared a raftsman.

The Captain of the front boat was urging, "More steam boys! Pour lamp oil on the wood."

"It's out," said another.

The two boats pounded and struggled with the muddy waters of the Big Sandy, and then the crowd on the forward boat yelled, "Captain Bromley, they're gaining on us!"

"That's all right; let 'em come," said Big Jim McCoy. "Our gunners can reach 'em!"

The old steamboat captain retorted: "Pass up a half dozen sides of that fat back bacon stacked on the tables, and feed it in the fire boxes. I'd rather this would be a boat race rather than a sea battle."

Soon the boiling fat of the bacon was sizzling and burning between the dry layers of wood which were constantly fed to the flame. The old *Fleetwing* began to master the mighty Sandy and it was plain to see that she was gaining on the *Mountain Boy,* which was heroically puffing and pounding to keep up. As they neared Louisa at the forks of the river, the old *Fleetwing* headed up the Leuvisa River with all the crowd yelling and shouting and firing their pistols, while the water foamed from the volley of bullets into the river and from both vessels. Just then the *Mountain Boy* hove up the Tug Fork, passing to the north of the little metropolis of the upper Sandy. So two level-headed steamboat captains, by the unnoticed sign language of the rivermen of their day, skillfully maneuvered their vessels into safe waters, each taking a different tributary of the stream, thus avoiding a close up sea battle and possible depletion of their passenger lists between two warring factions who were accustomed only to bushwhacking in the hills.

Chapter Twenty-One
Devil Anse Tracks
Peddler Murderer

Following the Civil War the people of that part of eastern Kentucky and southern West Virginia had nothing within their borders in the way of industrial development, except a little timbering and ginseng digging, until the latter part of the century when the first trunk line railroad came through. In those years previous to railroad transportation, most of the manufactured goods imported into this area came up the Ohio River from the industrial towns and cities where steamboating was the principal traffic. Above the point beyond which steamboats could pass, the pushboats carrying merchandise came up the Big Sandy and its tributaries. Such imported products were available mostly to people who lived along the larger water courses. The rest of the way up the creeks and over the hills and down the hollows, transportation was mostly done by horseback, since the narrow roads in most places did not accommodate horse-drawn vehicles. The traveling merchants and tradesmen known as "pack peddlers" carried on another mode of merchandising.

Immediately after the Civil War and up to the mid '80s, there were many Irish road merchants who carried their packs either on horseback or on their own backs. These were followed by other merchantmen strange to our mountain folk, men who ran far beyond the Mediterranean, merchants from the Near East, some Jewish and others Syrian. These affable strangers soon found a welcome at the cabins of the clever mountaineers. A great many of the hard-working travelers who carried their packs of ready-made goods from house to house throughout the mountains became successful, and as the industrial areas of the mountains were later developed these, like others, established their homes and businesses in the towns and cities which had sprung up in the last half century, and their descendants became successful citizens and blended into the way of life of the mountain people.

It was in the early days of September, in 1904, when two peddlers called at the gate of David James, where they rested for an hour and went in to eat a good meal. His home, known to trekkers as one of plenty (as mountain folks live), was a good place for travelers to stop as they went up and down the rocky roads.

There was an old abandoned log cabin just off the roadway a half-mile below the James home. As the two peddlers went on their way, a voice came from the door and said, "Come in; I want to buy a shirt."

One of the travelers kept on his way, thinking that there was some family living there in the dilapidated old building; his unfortunate partner turned aside and went through the broken gate toward the cabin door. While the first of the unsuspecting peddlers was resting in the shade of a chestnut tree some 300 yards down the creek awaiting the coming of his friend, he heard a shot in the direction of the old log house. Rushing back up to the place to find out the cause of the shooting, he found his partner dying with a bullet hole in his back and his head crushed by a heavy round stone.

Word spread up and down the creek and into all of the hollows where the neighbors lived, and one of them rode three miles farther up the creek to the home of Devil Anse Hatfield and told him of the murder. The old man mounted his horse and with rifle in hand, rode to the scene where a score of men and boys had gathered, all standing amazed and awe-stricken that such a thing could happen. A senseless murder and robbery had never been known in all of these parts before. The feudists had bushwhacked and shot each other, but nobody had ever been killed for his money around about here.

"We're glad you're here," said grizzled old Tom Chafin. "Yep, we know you can track them down, Anse, and nobody else here can do it like you."

Anse replied, "Has anybody gone into the woods yet?"

"No," said Uncle Tom.

"Well," said Anse, "Everybody stand back and stay where you are and let me figure this thing out."

The old bearded bear hunter studied a few moments, then began to inspect the ground as he looked in various directions. Soon he advanced toward the foot of the hill, and said, "Now don't let anybody come up any nearer behind me than ten steps. If I want you any closer, I'll let you come; but everybody stay back and follow me as I go. When I stop, you stop."

Six weeks later…

Judge Wilkinson called the court into session. The grand jury had returned all indictments. On the day of the trial of the accused young men, all witnesses had been called into the court by the bailiff, who stood at the window shouting their names as he looked over the crowd outside Logan Courthouse. The witnesses filed in, first among them a picturesque, broad-shouldered mountaineer with slouch hat, brown beard, hunting shirt, jean trousers and slip-on high top boots. It was Devil Anse.

"The court will now come to order. Are all parties ready for trial in this case?" asked Judge Wilkinson.

"Your Honor, on behalf of the state and as its attorney, I wish to announce that the state is, indeed, ready," the prosecuting attorney said.

Court: "What says the defense? As attorney for the defense, is the defense ready for trial."

"Your Honor, I introduce the first witness, Mr. Anderson Hatfield."

The witness was duly sworn and qualified and took the chair to testify on behalf of the state.

"Mr. Hatfield, I want you to tell the court and jury what you know about this case."

"Well, I was just picking apples when Greene Meadows came riding up the road and told me what had happened," Hatfield said. "I got on my horse and we rode back as quick as possible and found a group had gathered. It wasn't long till I looked over at the foot of the hill and saw what looked like fresh dirt where a body had made a quick step in going up the hill. I went up over a steep place and started along the point.

"I got down on my knees to look at the leaves where they had been stepped on and I laid aside the upper leaves, one at a time, that had been kicked up a little and the lower leaves next to the ground where it was solid showed that somebody had walked on them with big-headed tacks in their boots. I picked up one or two of these leaves and went on slow ahead and laid some other leaves away, and picked up the damp leaves next to the ground, and found where they had also been cut with shoe nails.

"I kept on following the tracks as I could tell by the leaves which had been cut with nails. After awhile I reached a hollow beech tree and I noticed two or three spots on the side of the tree as if somebody had rested his fingers on the side of the tree near the hollow place. The spots looked like they were from a man's fingers with blood on them. There were some pieces of dead wood piled up inside the hollow beech, and I reached in and took out a jeweler's case where peddlers carry rings and watches. You see, when a bear is running, his front toes cut deeper than when he is just walking on the leaves," he said.

Counsel for the defense: "We object, your Honor, what's bear hunting got to do with this case?"

Court: "Overruled. Let the witness continue."

"Yes, sir, I left that beech tree after I handed the boys the jeweler's case with the bloody handle, and I went on as I had, following the tracks through the leaves, and found where some sticks had been stepped on and had been freshly broken. I knowed I was pointed in the right direction. Then I comes to a rail fence and it was where no path had been before, and I saw where somebody had put their feet upon the fence rails and climbed over it. The tacks had cut little nicky-places on the rails, and they were fresh cut, just like bear claws.

"After I got over the fence and started around back of the fence through the timber, I saw weeds which had been parted like where somebody walks through. I also got down and picked up more leaves and got some more that were cut with shoe tacks. In going around a field I come to some dead logs where somebody had climbed over two or three of these logs and the tacks had scraped 'em. The other fellers were following me, and I told them to watch for the things that I was finding. Pretty soon I come to a rocky branch where there was a flat rock and somebody had stood on this rock not long before and left white specks on the rock where the shoe nails had made spots.

"I couldn't tell here whether they had gone up the hollow or down, so I looked down on some more flat rocks and saw where one had spit tobacco juice and it had sprangled toward down the hollow on the rock, so I knowed he was walking the way he spit. I followed on down over the rocks where the branch had run before it went dry, and there was two or three rocks which showed a step on each one which had a nail missing on the bottom of one foot about where the right big toe would be.

"I found another track on a rock further down which showed that one of the nails had been bent down and was cutting the rock with a little sharp groove and not striking on the head of the tack. After we got back to where the man was killed just about all of the boys and men in the whole neighborhood were gathered there and nobody seemed missing, so I figured that whoever done this trick was in the crowd, so Uncle Tom Chafin and me had all of them sit down on a long log, and we walked by and looked at the bottom of their feet as they held them up. It was Levi who had a nail missing on the sole of his shoe just under the big toe, and it was Jack who had a nail bent down on the toe of his foot where the edge of the nail had cut a long mark on the rock instead of a round mark.

"I should explain that after finding the foot specks on the rocks in the hollow, and before we got out of the woods, we kept on following the trail and the tobacco spit kept pointing in the direction of an old log house that stood up in the woods that had the roof nearly all off of it and the rain had beat in. I looked inside the door and I saw a board from the roof and a piece of board that had been moved. I knew the boards had been moved because the place under the boards where they had laid on the puncheon was a different color from the rest of the puncheon and the two boards had been laid over on the puncheon next to it. I raised the first puncheon on the old house floor and under it was hid a lot of bloody clothes. There were two pairs of pants, two jackets and two shirts."

Counsel for defense: "Your Honor, I want to move the Court to strike out the evidence of this witness as being immaterial, irrelevant and having no bearing upon this case. Why, your Honor, this witness has gone on the stand and told a bear-hunting story. What has that got to do with this case? How much is this court concerned with whether a bear has five toes or six or whether he cuts the leaves with his front claws deeper when he's running or when he's walking? The whole of this witness' testimony should be stricken out!"

Court: "This witness has clearly demonstrated that he has a long experience in woodcraft and that he has a keen insight into matters of which we are concerned. Without his experience as disclosed by this evidence, the state would not have any clue as to the identity of the guilty parties. He has qualified himself as being able not only to follow animals, but to follow human beings by the signs which they leave behind them, the tracks they make over leaves, stones, logs and fences, and can even tell you the way a man is traveling by the direction that his spit whizzes.

"This motion is overruled..."

Chapter Twenty-Two
Them Pestiferous Guineas

It was early in April, and Ansie had now become well-settled on his new farm across from Peter Creek and was all set for raising a big crop. In fact, the plowing with two yoke of oxen on one of the wide river bottoms was already in progress. The weather was unseasonably warm, and here and there the plum trees and apple blossoms were bursting forth. About midday members of the family spied a cavalcade of wagons slowly winding down the river. Settlers from beyond the mountains, toward the east, headed westward for the great open spaces. Some of the men and boys were walking, driving cattle, while the smaller children and women were loaded in the covered wagons whereever space was not taken by "house plunder" and such other personal belongings as were necessary to carry with them. The head wagon pulled up at the gate of Anse Hatfield, and the man on the driver's seat called for some good drinking water. Out came Ansie with a cheery, "How-do; won't you come in and have dinner?"

"No," replied the other, "We've et, but would like to get some good water."

"Well, you've found the best place in the country. I have the finest well water on this river, so get your vessels and draw all you need."

While the men gathered at the well, a pale lad who looked to be no more than a dozen years of age dropped listlessly down outside the picket fence. "That boy looks sick," said Anse.

"He isn't exactly well," replied the boss of the wagon train.

"I think he's homesick to return to his grandmother. His father and mother and all his other people are dead, except her. We have known him all his life and he wanted to go with us down the Ohio to the West. Now he's changed his mind and doesn't want to go ahead, and we have no way of sending him back home."

"Well," said the kindly faced mountaineer, without further thought, "He's got a home here if he wants it. I'd like to have a boy about his size. My boys are not big enough to be of much help, and I think this boy might be a good roustabout. What's your name, son?"

"Danny," replied the boy wanly.

"Ain't you hungry, son?"

"No, mister, but I'm wanting a drink of water terrible bad."

In a few moments a seven-year-old from inside came running up, and his father said, "Cappy, fetch that boy a gourd full of water; he' s punishing for a drink."

Soon the smaller boy returned from the well where water was being drawn and handed a long-neck gourd through the hole where a picket was missing, and the young traveler grasped it quickly and quenched his thirst from the cold, clear water.

The smaller boy put his head through the opening in the fence and said, "Danny, why don't you stay with us? Pap would be plum good to you and you would have a home here all the time." The blue eyes of the tired traveler brightened as he heard the welcoming voice of the little boy.

"Have you any brother?" asked the young stranger.

"Yeah, I got a brother—Johnsie; he's nine, and we've got two yearling calves with a yoke just made to fit, and we're learnin' them to pull a little sled, and we need somebody bigger than us to drive them!" It wasn't long until Johnsie came out, and he, too, begged the young man to stay a night or a month or for always.

Perhaps you have guessed what happened. The wagon train moved on down the river toward the West, and little Danny Christian had found a home with the Hatfields. Here began a life-long friendship between the little orphan boy and the two brothers with whom he was to make his home.

Mother Louvicey took the place of Danny's grandmother back in the mountains of Virginia where he had always lived. His tears were soon dried; he fell in love with everything that he found in his new home, and was given a place at the table between Cappy and Johnsie, his new brothers.

The next morning, Ansie continued his plowing with his two yoke of oxen down in the river bottom. When they turned out for dinner, he said, "Mother, I'm going to hef to do something with them limbfound guineas. Why, they're just scratching up everything I plant, and I'm not agonna to hev it!"

"Well, Ansie," said the little mother, "Why don't you send them to the neighbors up on Peter Creek. Davey Mounts and the McCoy neighbors said they'd like to have some guinea hens."

"Well, they can just have every pesky one on this place; I'll send them up in the morning bright and early!"

Early the next morning, young Danny and the little Hatfields got out the yearlings and loaded up the sled with big hickory baskets full of guinea fowls, securing the tops so they couldn't escape; then the boys struck out for the creek across the river, where the clacking birds were distributed among all the neighbors. Johnsie cautioned: "Pap said to tell you to keep watch on all these guineas up until they git used to your place, because he wants you to have them and he don't want them coming back."

At daybreak on the following morning, Ansie was back in his fields plowing and planting with a sense of satisfaction that he would not be pestered with the guineas any longer. Suddenly he looked across toward the mouth of the big Kentucky creek where the neighbors' adjoining fences could be seen for a distance of more than a mile as the rails zig-zagged up the creek parallel to the road, when to his surprise he saw all of the guinea fowls, runnin' like a blue streak, traveling the winding fence road in his direction. Assembling on the opposite side of the river, it appeared that by one signal they all arose and flew across the river, alighted on the fence and began calling out a big welcome to their original owner.

At dinner time he told Louvicey how he had seen them winding down the creek like a marching army, and when they lit on his side, what made him so mad was that they began to taunt: "Got back! Got back! Got back!"

Chapter Twenty-Three
Neighborly Corn Hoeing

The casual reader who seldom hears anything from the hill people except what he sees in flaming headlines about the eruption of some ancient feud or that a mountaineer has bushwhacked his neighbor over a sandy hog, might be led to believe that little goes on in the hill country except feuding, fussing and fighting. Little is told of the neighborliness and brotherly kindness of even the meanest of the feudists, such as along about June, when they grab their corn hoes and meet at the home of a neighbor to work out the corn.

For six miles up and down the creek early one morning, for example, all the men and boys were seen carrying their corn hoes and converging upon the farm of widow Phoebe Mounts, who came out the front door, shading her eyes with her hand, and said, "Land sakes, Anse Hatfield, why are all you boys comin' here so early with your corn hoes?'"

"That's just it, Aunt Phoebe, we've come for the 'land's sake' and for your sake, to hoe out your corn crop today. We vowed your corn was rennin' away in the weeds, and you wasn't able to hoe it out since Bill died, so we have all come to give you a hand. If all these wall-eyed rascals don't hoe out your corn before the day's over, I'll beat everyone of them to death!"

"Why, land sakes, land sakes, Anse, you all are just so clever to come down and save my corn from the weeds!"

"All right," said Anse, "Pitch in, men, and line out here. Ellison, you claim to be the best man with the hoe anywhere in the country. You take the first row. Dave, you and Pete and Bill fall in next, and all the rest of you follow and let's get this job done for this good woman." So began the rattling and scraping of the old hickory-handled rim fire hoes down through the river bottom and around the rocky hillside.

Just as it had all been planned, about midday all the grown gals started coming in from their homes with big hickory-slat baskets full of grub. When it was spread out under the shady apple trees near the open bucket well, Mary Chafin grabbed the dinner horn and began to blow for the hungry corn hoers who were spread out through the fields and up the hollows, where their ringing hoes had slashed the weeds and cleared the corn fields.

Then they came at the sound of the cow horn and threw down their hats, rolled up their sleeves, and washed up at the creek branch, then sat down in the shade to get ready to eat their grub—cornbread, mutton, buttermilk, and plenty of garden sass.

"Listen, Dick and Sam," said Anse, "the rest of us can finish Aunt Phoebe's work today. So after you eat, I want you two men to take your hosses on down and start plowin' ol' cripple Jim Cline's corn, because we're all goin' to meet at his place in the mornin' and have another workin' day— and there's plenty of other jobs to do between now and Saturday night. At that time, I want all you fiddlers and banjo pickers to meet up at the mouth of Barren-She Creek where there'll be a big frolic, with plenty to eat and drink. So hurry boys, and dig in; we've got lots to do!"

Chapter Twenty-Four
Hatfield Pioneers

The following account was first penned in 1952 by Coleman A. Hatfield, son of Cap Hatfield and father of Coleman C. Hatfield. At the time of this writing, C.A. Hatfield, as he was often called, was a practicing attorney in Logan County. This chapter was written as a short synopsis of Hatfield family history to be used in conjunction with a publication celebrating the centennial of the City of Logan, West Virginia. Several of the details that he discusses here, such as the Shawnee Indian raid, the killing of David Musick, and the blood-thirsty raiders crossing the state borders, are discussed in earlier chapters in greater detail. The story is included in this volume as an overview—described in broad strokes—of the Hatfield story as documented by a grandson of Devil Anse Hatfield. It also adds a certain amount of color to the Hatfield family story and the feud era.

About the year 1800, the territory of out of which Logan County was carved was a vast wilderness and hunting ground of the red men.

Earlier, in the year 1792, a band of Shawnee Indians raided the white settlements of the Clinch River and killed a settler named David Musick at what is now Honaker, in Russell County, Virginia. Musick's widow and five children were carried away by Indians but were subsequently overtaken by a party of white men who rescued them. One of the rescuers was Ephraim Hatfield, a young settler of Thompson's Creek, now in New Garden District. Some two years before that time, Ephraim's wife, Mary Smith Hatfield, had died, leaving two small sons, Joseph and Valentine.

Sometime after the rescue of the Musick family, Ephraim Hatfield and the widow, Anna Musick, were married and, like many other sturdy pioneers, set out to with their families across the mountain toward the Sandy River country, and settled on Blackberry Creek in Pike County, Kentucky, not many miles from the present city of Matewan, West Virginia.

The second son, Valentine, later became known as "Wall" Hatfield, who settled on Tug Rover at the present site of Sprigg in the county of Mingo.

"Uncle Wally," as he was known in later years, reared his family of twelve children, among whom was the second Ephraim. "Big Eph," as he was often called, was born in 1811 and settled on Mate Creek. He became a mighty hunter and once killed a panther with a hunting knife on a rocky hilltop at the head of Mud Lick Branch near Red Jacket.

"Panther Killer" Ephraim's second son, Anderson, was born in 1839 and became the captain in a company of a Virginia militia, which trained in Logan from 1856 until 1860. Anderson entered the Southern Army under the command of General Alfred Beckley and early earned a fighting name of "Devil Anse" Hatfield.

Following the Civil War, "Devil Anse" took up a tract of approximately five thousand acres of land on the north side Tug Fork of Sandy, near the mouth of Peter Creek. He lived there for some fifteen years when local warfare broke out, which has been later known as the Hatfield and McCoy feud. A river that marked the boundary between the states of West Virginia and Kentucky became the deadline, across which it was unsafe for any enemy to pass.

Much has been written and many stories have been exaggerated regarding the conflict that lasted during the 1880s. There were approximately one hundred fifty men who participated at various times and places in the pitched battles along the border. Invading parties from both families would often ride across the line into enemy territory where bloodshed would result. Governors of the two states refused to honor extradition papers for the participants living in the opposing state, it being charged that the sovereignty of both states had been violated by outsiders in quest of the scalps of their enemies.

Few are living who remember the clashes of galloping raiders across the border of seventy years ago. The Hatfields and McCoys alike, as well as their neighbors whose ancestors had come into these rugged hills a hundred years before the feud days, have all come from the pioneer stock who pushed the frontier of civilization across the hills.

Marooned in the wilderness, they engaged in the struggle of subduing the forest and establishing homes for their families. The patriarch settlers established homes for their sons and daughters around the old homestead, so that it is easy to understand how large families developed in many areas with their kith and kin who held the frontier prior to the great industrial development of the century, including mines, highways, schools and churches.

Chapter Twenty-Five
Hatfield-McCoy Feud

Excerpt by G.T. Swain,
from *The History Of Logan County*, 1927

Dr. Coleman C. Hatfield elected to include the former chapter, *Hatfield Pioneers*, and the following account in this work, for he felt that these two writings have a certain amount of relevance to documenting the feud era. In this partiocular case, it is largely due to G. T. Swain's journalistic abilities and his heavy leaning on the earlier work of Henry Clay Ragland that make the account especially relevant. At the time of this writing, in 1927, Swain was a senior reporter for the local newspaper, *The Logan County Banner*, in the City of Logan, WV. He was well acquainted with most of the individuals directly involved in the Hatfield-McCoy feud. Ragland, Swain's mentor and Logan County's most prolific historian, was an attorney who first came to the area shortly after the War Between the States. During the skirmish he was a Confederate major serving on Stonewall Jackson's personal staff. After settling down in Logan, he eventually became owner and publisher of *The Logan County Banner*.

In 1882 there occurred on Tug River, in Logan County, now Mingo County, West Virginia, events that continued through many years that gave this section of the state more notoriety than any other thing that ever transpired within the bounds of the county. It was during this year that the Hatfield-McCoy feud blazed up, which was destined to last for many years.

Authors and newspaper writers all over the nation have seized upon the events of this unfortunate feud to draw vivid and lurid tales of what transpired, without adhering strictly to truth. It seems that it has been the unanimous custom of writers to picture the Hatfields as bloodthirsty desperadoes and rather weave a halo about the heads of the McCoys.

Permit this writer to state, early in the beginning, that he will not undertake to defend either the Hatfields or the McCoy family for, perhaps, they were both to blame in many respects; but for the sake of truth, without partiality or color, an attempt will here be made to give the cold facts as they have been gathered after an exhaustive investigation during which much of this information was gleaned from living actors who participated in this unfortunate feud.

The contending factions in this internecine strife lived on opposite sides of Tug River, a small stream that separates West Virginia from Kentucky. During those days Logan County, West Virginia, and Pike County, Kentucky, the scenes of this bloody feud, were sparsely settled, wild and mountainous sections. Mountaineers through whose veins flowed the purest Anglo-Saxon blood populated the territory. They were among the early pioneers of this section and were noted for their hospitality, courage, steadfastness and love of personal liberty.

First, the reader must bear in mind that we had no organized police forces during those days such as we have now. Sheriffs had few deputies and they were charged with the duty of collecting meager taxes more than enforcing the law. Then, it must be remembered that mountain people rarely sought redress for wrongs at the hands of the law, but settled their difficulties in the good old-fashioned way — with their fists — and after personal quarrels were vindicated in this manner the hatchet was buried and all was well.

Randall McCoy, the leader of the McCoy clan, lived on Blackberry Branch of Pond Creek, in Pike County, Kentucky. Just across the river, on the West Virginia side, lived Anderson Hatfield, later dubbed "Devil Anse," the leader of the Hatfield faction. Some writers have stated that trouble between these factions date back to the Civil War, but such is not the case.

"Devil Anse" Hatfield served through the war on the Confederate side with distinction. He was noted for his bravery and rendered valiant service to the "Lost Cause." The McCoys were likewise enlisted in the Confederate cause. The fact that these families intermarried and were extensively related disproves the statement that enmity existed since the civil strife.

A few razor-backed hogs—long-legged and sharp-nosed porkers—played a part in the beginning of the trouble. In those days every farmer had a number of porkers and it was the custom to mark the pigs when quite young by cutting a slit of some description in their ears and turning them loose in the mountains where they could fatten on the abundant mast to be found and, late in the fall, the owner would round up his hogs and drive them into his home to be slaughtered.

Some time during the seventies one Floyd Hatfield drove a number of hogs from the forests and confined them in a pen at Stringtown, the pen being located by the roadside near his home. A few days later Ran'l McCoy passed that way and stopped his horse to see the hogs. McCoy dismounted and examined the porkers and claimed them as his property. It is probable that Floyd Hatfield and Ran'l McCoy had used the same symbol in marking their property while they were yet pigs, and it is barely possible that an owner, who had never seen the hogs since, could recognize them months later after they had fattened and grown to maturity.

But McCoy claimed the property and brought a civil action for their recovery, as he should have done. The date of the trial arrived. Valentine Hatfield, justice of the peace, at Raccoon Hollow, held Court. Naturally, relatives of both parties attended the trial in large numbers. The justice impaneled a jury and every opportunity was given both parties to present their claims. Ran'l McCoy made an impassioned speech to the jury, openly charging several of Hatfield's witnesses with perjury. One of these witnesses was Bill Staton, brother-in-law to Floyd Hatfield, who, incensed by the charge, attempted to strike his traducer, but was prevented by McCoy's son.

McCoy lost the case, and there it should have ended. They had a fair and impartial hearing and the jury decided against McCoy's claim. But McCoy returned to his home in a vindictive mood, grumbling and threatening.

Time passed on until 1880, when Bill Staton met Paris and Sam McCoy a mile below what is now known as Hatfield Tunnel, on the Norfolk & Western Railroad. Each knew that bad feeling existed and Staton rightly guessed that the McCoy brothers would show him no mercy. He leaped behind a bush, broke off the top, and rested his gun in a fork of two limbs, took deadly aim and fired. Paris McCoy fell and, although severely wounded in the hip, he gained his feet and shot Staton in the breast. Weapons were then tossed aside by both parties and they came together in a fierce hand-to-hand combat.

The fight was one of the most ferocious ever known. Weakened by the loss of blood and suffering excruciating pain, they fought on until Paris McCoy was about to succumb to the superior strength of his powerful adversary, when Sam McCoy, armed with a pistol, came up and sent a ball crashing through the brain of Staton, who fell back with his arms tightly wound about the body of his adversary and instantly expired. He was wrenched loose from Paris McCoy and left to die in the roadway. His body was not found until some days later.

Any bad feeling that might have existed between the Hatfields and the McCoys at this time did not sway the hand of justice, for suspicion at once pointed to the McCoy brothers. Paris promptly surrendered and was given a trial before Magistrate Valentine Hatfield and released from custody. Sam McCoy fled to the hills, but after eluding officers for a month or more, was captured by Elias Hatfield, an officer of the law, who did not mistreat him but confined him in jail, after which he was indicted by a grand jury of his county, tried and acquitted.

In the summer of 1882 it happened a relative of both parties ran for office and was supported by both Hatfields and McCoys. Both of these factions met on August 7, to work in harmony for their candidate. It was the custom in those days, and for many years later, to supply voters with copious quantities of whiskey. This occasion was no exception to the rule and all participants imbibed freely of the fluid that dethrones reason and makes beasts out of many good men.

As is the case in many instances when men fill themselves with bad whiskey, things long forgotten arise in the minds of drunken men, and Tolbert McCoy, on this occasion, approached Elias Hatfield and demanded payment of an old debt. A quarrel ensued and the fight was on, with others of both factions standing by and letting the participants settle their differences. Elias Hatfield got the worst of it. After the fight was over, Ellison Hatfield challenged the victorious Tolbert McCoy to fight a man more of his size. With true mountain courage McCoy accepted the challenge but the battle soon went against him. At this stage of the fight McCoy did a cowardly deed.

Although no weapons had been used in either of the fights, McCoy resorted to his knife when he saw he was being whipped and plunged the blade into the body of Hatfield repeatedly and with frightful effect. Though horribly slashed and spurting blood from many wounds, Hatfield stood his ground and continued to fight fair. Throwing McCoy to the ground, he sat down upon him while McCoy yet plunged the knife into his body. Seizing a huge stone, Hatfield raised it above his head when Pharmer McCoy, who had been patiently waiting the opportunity, shot Hatfield and rolled him from the body of his brother and Hatfield lay fatally wounded in his gore. During the course of the fight, Randolph McCoy Jr., a youth of fifteen, had stabbed Hatfield several times.

As soon as Pharmer McCoy saw the effect of his shot, he dropped his weapon and fled. He was pursued by Constable Floyd Hatfield and captured. Tolbert and young Randolph were also arrested on the spot. Hatfield was removed to the home of one of his relatives where efforts were made to save his life. The prisoners remained on the election grounds, under heavy guard, for some hours. Then they were taken to the home of Johns Hatfield for the night. They were in charge of Tolbert Hatfield and Joseph Hatfield, two justices of the peace in Pike County, Kentucky. The officers permitted Ran'l McCoy, the father, to remain with the sons all night.

The next morning the officers started with their prisoners to Pikeville, the county seat. While on the way they were overtaken by Val Hatfield and Elias Hatfield, who demanded that the prisoners be returned to the magisterial district where the fight had occurred, which was legal, for trial and to await the result of the wounds suffered by Ellison Hatfield. Ran'l McCoy traveled on to Pikeville. After turning back, the party was joined by Charles Carpenter, "Devil Anse" Hatfield, Johnson Hatfield and Alexander Messer. As precautionary measures, the prisoners were taken across the river and dinner was given them at the home of Rev. Anderson Hatfield.

The prisoners were taken to an old house and kept under heavy guard, those performing this duty being Alex Messer, Johns Hatfield, "Devil Anse" and Val Hatfield, Charles Carpenter, Joseph Murphy, Dock Mayhorn, Plyant Mayhorn, Selkirk McCoy and his two sons, Albert and L. D., Lark and Anderson Varney, Dan Whitt, Elijah Mounts, and others. Along toward night the mother of the prisoners and the wife of Tolbert McCoy arrived on the scene. After being permitted to talk to the prisoners the women left and stayed at a nearby house until morning, when they returned and found the prisoners unharmed. It is recorded that someone addressed them and said: "If Ellison Hatfield dies we are going fill the prisoners full of holes."

A report reached those guarding the prisoners that Ran'l McCoy was assembling a crowd to rescue his sons. Double precaution was taken by the guards to prevent the prisoners from being taken from custody. On the afternoon of August 9, the third day since the fight, word reached the guards that Ellison was dead. Fearing that public sentiment in that section would be too strong against their charges, the officers left the scene at 9 o'clock and started for the Pikeville County jail, at Pikeville.

Shortly after crossing the river they were overtaken by a mob and the prisoners taken from the officers. It is recorded by some biographers that the prisoners were tied to bushes and Alex Messer is said to have fired six shots into the head of Pharmar McCoy. Ellison Mounts is reported to have shot Tolbert McCoy and some one of the party killed Randolph McCoy Jr. It is likewise recorded that Val Hatfield remained on the West Virginia side of Tug River and when the mob formed he begged them to let the law take its course.

Of course the names of the perpetrators of the crime were not immediately known, hence when the coroner's jury met the next day they returned a verdict that the McCoys came to their death at the hands of persons unknown. Later on twenty-three members of the Hatfield faction were indicted in the Pike County (Kentucky) Circuit Court, each charged with three murders. The indictments were returned into court on the 14th day of September 1882, but none of them were tried until seven years later.

Blood flows thicker than water. In those days, to offer an insult to a person was to strike every one of his relatives. They were bound together by bonds of blood relationship that would stand the test of fire. However, the feud subsided to some extent, with an occasional flare-up between some of the younger men of the factions. In 1886 an incident occurred to fan the smoldering flames again. One Jeff McCoy was accused of murdering Fred Walford, in Kentucky, and McCoy fled and sought refuge in the home Johns Hatfield on the West Virginia side. Johns Hatfield had married a sister of McCoy. Hatfield had long since refused to take any part in trouble between the factions.

Near Johns Hatfield lived Cap Hatfield who had in his employ one Wallace. The Hatfield faction felt that there was a spy in their community due to the reports that kept reaching the McCoy clan. They desired peace, but these reports kept fanning the old flames and the McCoys were sending back threats. Through that strange and mysterious medium by which news travels in the mountainous regions, known as the "grapevine" method, reports flew thick and fast. Some of the friends of the Hatfields finally accused a Daniels woman of being the spy, and a mob visited her house one night and gave her a thrashing. Mrs. Daniels was the sister of Jeff McCoy.

Jeff McCoy, who was at the time hiding at the home of Johns Hatfield, reached the conclusion that this man Wallace was the instigator and leader of the outrage perpetrated upon his sister. He vowed to kill him and, accompanied by a friend, he visited the home of Cap Hatfield on November 17, 1886, when he knew Cap Hatfield was absent and Mrs. Hatfield lay ill in bed. Wallace was busy working in the yard of the home when McCoy and his friend rode up, drew their weapons and commanded Wallace to surrender. McCoy pretended to arrest him for the purpose of taking him to Pikeville.

Wallace knew his captors would show no mercy him and they had hardly left the Hatfield home when Wallace made a break for liberty. He was shot down but gained his feet and succeeded in reaching the Hatfield home, secured weapons and drove his enemies off after they had poured shot after shot through the house while Mrs. Hatfield lay ill in bed.

Cap Hatfield returned home and was told of the attack. Hatfield had been appointed special constable and he advised Wallace to swear out a warrant for Jeff McCoy and his friend, Hurley. This was done and the papers given Cap Hatfield to serve. Single-handed he went after the pair, although he knew them to be dangerous and armed to the teeth. With his accustomed coolness he covered them with his gun, ordered Hurley to throw his weapon on the ground and then disarmed McCoy. He started for Logan Courthouse to place his men in jail. While on the way McCoy broke and run and succeeded in reaching the river which he swam and refused to heed the call of the officer to halt. As he reached the opposite shore a shot from the officer's gun brought the fleeing fugitive down, a dead man. In the excitement Hurley escaped.

Wallace was captured the next spring by Dud and Jake McCoy, brothers of Jeff McCoy, and taken to jail at Pikeville. A short time later he succeeded in escaping. He went to Virginia, and the McCoys offered a heavy reward for his capture. A short time later, two men reached the McCoy neighborhood and claimed the reward. Where was the prisoner? The answer was given by the exhibition of a bloody lock of hair.

The reward was paid.

Although the Hatfields visited the Kentucky side of the river quite often, having business that called them there, they were not arrested, although indictments were pending against them. But in 1887, Governor Proctor Knott of Kentucky was prevailed upon to offer a huge reward for their capture. His successor, General Simon Bolivar Buckner, renewed the rewards and issued requisitions for those indicted. He appointed one Frank Phillips to visit the Governor of West Virginia and present his requisition papers.

Many writers have felt inclined to paint Phillips as a hero and as brave a man as ever trod the soil of Kentucky. Of his bravery there can be no question. He was slight of stature, but while he was brave as a lion he was equally as heartless, and many times he has been known to stop innocent people upon the highway and make them dance, from which he seemed to derive much amusement as he shot into the ground near their feet.

To deliver those indicted to Frank Phillips, to be returned to Kentucky, with the meager police protection that could have been offered them, would have been similar to leading a lamb to slaughter. All the McCoy's and their friends were in Pike County, Kentucky, and they were almost the total inhabitants. It would have been necessary to take the Hatfields and their friends to Pikeville, and Governor Wilson was made acquainted with these facts.

In addition, the McCoys had committed felonies in West Virginia and Governor Wilson could have, with equal propriety and equal legal rights, demanded their surrender to West Virginia authorities. No indictments had been lodged against the Hatfields or their friends in West Virginia that had not been served. They had been haled into court many times and fined for carrying revolvers and like misdemeanors. In the early days of the feud R. W. Peck was Sheriff of Logan County, with J. E. Peck and J. A. Peck as his efficient deputies. They had a tremendous territory to cover. J. R. Henderson followed Peck as law enforcement officer in the county during the later period of the feud. Ira J. Maginnis of Huntington presided over the Circuit Court and he was followed by Judge T. H. Harvey of the same place.

But Governor Simon Buckner was high-tempered and rode a high horse. He felt that his commands were law. On Governor Wilson's refusal to honor the requisition he grew exceedingly wroth and a salty correspondence followed. Back and forth flew official correspondence which grew more bitter each day.

Feeling that he was clothed with all the authority needed, Frank Phillips, in company of three others, crossed the river with the intention of kidnapping any of those whom they could find that were implicated in the feud and taking them into Kentucky. They suddenly came upon Selkirk McCoy, Tom Chambers and Mose Christian, three of those charged with the slaying of the McCoy brothers. They were arrested by the quartette from Kentucky and hurried across Tug River and taken to the jail in Pikeville. The rage of the Hatfield faction knew no bounds. They saw State rights trampled under feet. They saw their homes invaded without rights, they saw their personal liberty gone, and it is little wonder they then resolved to invoke the old Mosaic law, "an eye for and eye and a tooth for a tooth." If they were not secure under the protection of the State law from invaders from another State, they would prepare to defend themselves and also make their enemies pay the penalty.

There can be no doubt but what the actions of Frank Phillips, impulsive and with utter disregard for legal rights, prolonged the feud for many years. Members of the Hatfield faction gathered and decided they would take reprisal methods against the McCoy's, for which Phillips was so active. At midnight, January 1, 1888, a band of men crossed Tug River and surrounded the home of Ran'l McCoy, recognized leader of the McCoy clan. The house was a double log structure, a passage separating the two buildings. The torch was applied to the home and shots fired through the doors and windows.

Ran'l McCoy and Calvin McCoy seized guns and fired upon those on the outside. Allifair McCoy opened a door and received a shot through the breast at the hands of Ellison Mounts. Allifair's mother rushed to her aid and was knocked insensible by Jim Vance. The two McCoy men then fled from the burning building and endeavored to reach a corncrib, but Calvin was shot and fell dead at the door of the crib. Ran'l McCoy fled from the building and in the darkness of the night disappeared from view. Newspapers from all over the nation seized upon this raid and pictured it in the most lurid colors.

Frank Phillips, who has been pictured by feature writers as such a doughty hero, took upon himself the responsibility of bringing the perpetrators to the bar of justice. Without any legal authority or consent of the States of West Virginia or Kentucky, he formed a band of men and crossed the border of West Virginia on another kidnapping raid.

On January 8, 1888, Jim Vance, an elderly man, and Cap Hatfield, who was then a comparatively young man, left their friends near the Guyandotte River and went to the home of Vance on Tug River. On their way to visit Vance's home they had the good fortune to kill two coons, which they carried over with them.

On their arrival Mrs. Jim Vance cooked the coons and they ate the meat. The next day they started on their return journey and while climbing Thacker Mountain, with Mrs. Vance probably a hundred yards in front of the two men as a scout, the woman was horrified to find a body of men ascending the other side of the mountain on horses, and she immediately recognized them as the enemies of the Hatfield faction.

Fleeing back down the mountainside to her husband's side, she told Vance and Cap Hatfield of their precarious situation. Vance, who was ill from eating too much of the coon meat, immediately declared he would not flee, but was going to stand his ground and shoot it out with the band.

He and Hatfield took refuge behind some trees and for several minutes they held their enemies at bay. However, a flank movement by the Phillips party enabled one of them to shoot Vance, inflicting a fatal wound, and the latter advised Cap Hatfield to make his escape. Hatfield was able to do this by dodging from tree to tree until he was out of range of the guns of the Phillips party, when he secured a horse and fled across the mountain ranges until he reached the Hatfield fortress at the mouth of Huff's Creek.

In the meantime Vance had continued to fire until he became so weak from loss of blood that he was unable to pull the trigger of his rifle. It is said that Frank Phillips advanced on the wounded man and Vance, with one supreme effort, tried hard to press the trigger of his pistol and, as he did so, Phillips sent a bullet crashing through his brain and Vance fell back dead.

But Phillips had failed to quench this thirst for blood. Organizing another small army of men, he again crossed the border, but due to the reliable old "grapevine telephone," their coming was known and preparations had been made for their reception.

About January 18, 1888, they met on Grapevine Creek. The Kentuckians outnumbered the West Virginians, but they were taken by surprise. Phillips and his men retreated behind a stone fence and poured volley after volley into the defense of the Hatfield faction. After two hours and fifteen minutes of fighting the Hatfield faction retreated, leaving William Dempsey dead upon the field. Among those of the Hatfield faction who were wounded were Tom Mitchell, "Indian" Hatfield and Lee White. Bud McCoy suffered the most severe injuries among the Phillips men, but others suffered minor casualties. This was the last serious fight between the different factions.

Feeling they would never find peace in their home neighborhood, many of the Hatfields came to Logan Courthouse and appealed for protection. Being unable to furnish the necessary protection, which would have required a small standing army, patrolling the border for many months, officials in Logan persuaded the Hatfields and their friends to secrete themselves on Blair Mountain, where they remained for many days while the feud died down.

Significant is the fact that Governor Wilson had sent an emissary here to ascertain the true facts of the feud, and he was in the Hatfield neighborhood when Phillips and his crowd crossed the river and attacked the Hatfields. William Floyd was the emissary and he witnessed the battle on Grapevine Creek. Other trouble that occurred later took place in Mingo County, for in 1895 Mingo was separated from Logan.

Leaving the banks of Tug River, "Devil Anse" and Cap Hatfield removed their families to Main Island Creek, where they have since spent a peaceful life, "Devil Anse" dying a peaceful death on January 6, 1921. The large number who attended his burial attest, in a measure, the love and esteem in which his neighbors in this section of the county held him. Loving relatives and friends have erected at his grave a marble replica of the famous old mountaineer, an admirable likeness of the man, the monument having been made in Italy by a famous sculptor and brought here at an enormous cost.

The battle at Grapevine Creek was the last serious fight between these two factions. In this battle Bud McCoy, of the McCoy faction, was severely wounded. Among the Hatfield clan Tom Mitchell, "Indian" Hatfield and Lee White received wounds. Frank Phillips and his party continued for some time making forays into West Virginia and succeeded in capturing nine of the Hatfield clan, whom they landed in jail at Pikeville.

In the meantime the quarrel between the Governor of Kentucky and the chief executive of West Virginia continued. The correspondence between them was exceedingly pithy and acrimonious. Later on the prisoners captured by Phillips and his party were removed to Louisville jail pending trial. A great legal battle followed. General P. Watt Hardin and former Governor Proctor Knott ably represented Kentucky. The best counsel of West Virginia represented the interest of this State. Phillips was charged with kidnapping citizens of another State and was taken in charge by a United States marshal. The case came to trial in the United States Circuit Court for the District of Kentucky and Phillips, on the stand, assumed the responsibility for all his acts, and exonerated Governor Buckner, who was openly charged with complicity in the kidnapping, from any connivance therewith. The Court, Judge Barr presiding, ruled that the Court had no jurisdiction and the prisoners were returned to Pike County to be tried in the Circuit Court there for their crimes.

At their trial, Ellison Mounts was sentenced to hang for the murder of Allifair McCoy, a comely maid who was brutally murdered when her home was burned, as related in the former pages, while Johns Hatfield, Valentine Hatfield and Plyant Mayhorn and others were convicted and sentenced to the Kentucky State penitentiary for life.

Ellison Mounts made an appeal to have his sentenced commuted on the ground that he had pleaded guilty and, therefore, he should be sentenced to the penitentiary for life instead of hanging. However, on February 19, 1890, he was hanged. A few days later a letter was received by Anderson Hatfield, at his home in West Virginia, in which was enclosed a small piece of the rope with which Mounts had been hanged, and the latter was addressed to "Devil Anse" Hatfield, hence we have

THIS PISTOL is believed to have once belonged to Anse, and eventually ended up in the West Virginia archives collection. He owned a variety of pistols, rifles and shotguns over his lifetime. — The collection of the West Virginia State Archives

the origin of how that feudist obtained his nom de plume. The appellation stuck with him through life.

Johns Hatfield was tried at Prestonsburg, Kentucky, in 1898, for complicity in killing three of the McCoys, and sentenced to the penitentiary for life. While serving time there he saved the life of the warden of the penitentiary when that official was attacked by a negro, armed with a fork. The burly negro, of giant size, had thrown the warden to the floor and was stabbing him in the neck with the sharpened fork when Hatfield ran up and grappled with the negro, throwing the latter to the floor, but the negro arose and was about to overcome the strength of Hatfield when the latter succeeded in getting hold of a pen knife with which he slashed the jugular vein of the negro and the latter quickly bled to death.

The rescue of the warden won for Hatfield popular favor with the penitentiary officials and they immediately started a movement to have Hatfield pardoned, which was done by Governor Beckham, six years after Hatfield had entered the institution.

A few little skirmishes took place after this but the feud gradually died down. The hills and valleys that once rang with the report of pistols and rifles, and whose soil was bathed with human blood, is now stilled in peace. Of the participants who yet live, the seed of hatred and animosity has been purged from their hearts and they are now law abiding, peaceful citizens. Cap Hatfield, one of the leaders of the Hatfield faction, is now a Deputy Sheriff of Logan County, and assisting in enforcing the law. Those days of lawlessness and strife are gone forever and not one of the living actors would ever have it to return. As they draw near to the evening tide of life, they would like to blot from memory's pages those dreadful dark days of strife, and look to better deeds, so that when the Death Angel comes he will find their souls at peace with the world, and many good deeds registered on the credit side of life's ledger when the Great Judge shall pass upon our lives for the good we have done while here on earth.

MAIN STREET, in downtown Logan in 1910. The business district was developing rapidly during this time period. Overnight, the growing coal and timber industry made Logan a bustling community.

LOGAN COUNTY Courthouse in 1917. Its mammoth, post Civil War design became the landmark for the county.

Back, Mossie Caudwell Hatfield, Chrissie Hatfield Lilly and, front, Nancy Hatfield, holding Tom Lilly. — The Coleman C. Hatfield Collection

DEVIL ANSE Hatfield is shown with his two pet black bears. Visitors often came to the homeplace to see the animals. — The Coleman C. Hatfield Collection

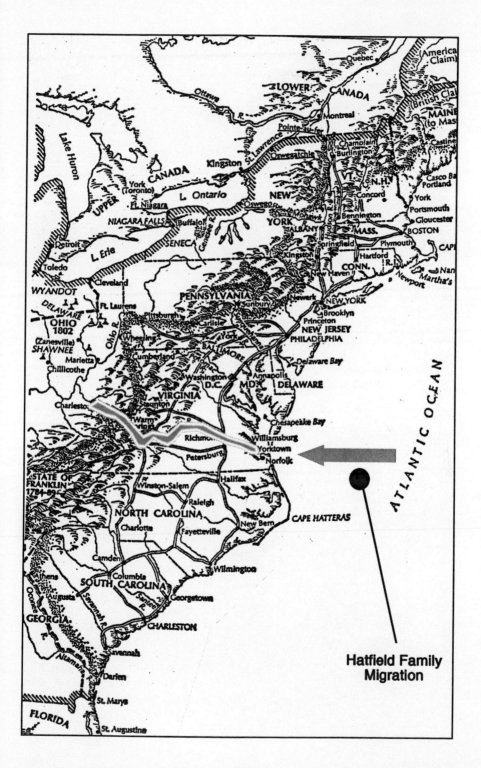

Hatfield Family
Migration

THE ANDERSON "Devil Anse" Hatfield family came together for this famous family portrait in front of a Beech Fork cabin. Being heavily armed, the Hatfields must have seemed threatening and prepared for conflict to onlookers. In this and other family photos of the time period, many of the small children also held weapons. Front row, left to right: Tennyson (Tennis) Hatfield (son of Anderson), Levicy Hatfield (daughter of Johnse),Willis Hatfield (son of Anderson), and "Watch" or "Yellow Watch," Devil Anse' hunting dog. Second row: Mrs. Mary Hensley-Simpkins-Howes, (daughter of Anderson) with daughter Vici Simpkins, William Anderson "Devil Anse"

Hatfield, Louvicey (also, Levicy or Visey) Chafin Hatfield (wife of Anderson), Nancy Elizabeth Hatfield (wife of Cap) with son Robert Elliott Hatfield, Louise Hatfield (daughter of Cap), Cap Hatfield, and Coleman Hatfield (son of Cap). Top row: Rosa Lee Hatfield (daughter of Anderson), Detroit (Troy) Hatfield (son of Anderson), Betty Hatfield (Caldwell) (daughter of Anderson), Elias Hatfield (son of Anderson), Tom Chafin (nephew of William Anderson), Joe D. Hatfield (son of William Anderson), Ock Damron, Shephard Hatfield (son of Cap), Levicy Emma Hatfield (daughter of Cap), and Bill Border, store clerk. — The collection of the West Virginia State Archives

OCK DAMRON, Devil Anse Hatfield, Jim Vance (with saddlebags) and W. B. Borden, who arranged the photograph session, pose along a rock wall. Devil Anse was an excellent marksman and was at home in the outdoors. — The collection of the West Virginia State Archives

AT LEFT, it is believed that this particular photo was one of a series of publicity shots taken to promote an early silent film. A short movie was eventually filmed to depict the Hatfield and McCoy fued, and Devil Anse signed on to appear in the project. The film's limited theatrical release was never deemed a box office success.

Unfortunately for historians, no film reels have survived the many decades since this photo was taken. — The collection of the West Virginia State Archives

GLARING INTO the camera lens, Devil Anse Hatfield could look intimidating to others, especially if angered or his family was challenged. He was an accomplished Confederate Civil War veteran; he was also a crackshot who was willing to aggressively defend his family if trouble erupted. Even so, he was well liked in Mingo and Logan County and had many friends and acquaintances. At the time this photo was taken, he was already well known due to feud coverage published in national newspapers. — The collection of the West Virginia State Archives

THIS CRINKLED and faded photograph of Devil Anse Hatfield was taken years after the feud violence had ceased. It was most likely taken at a studio in Logan, WV. — The collection of the West Virginia State Archives

THE DEVIL, the Hatfield family patriarch, poses with an unknown gentleman during the later years of his life. Some historians have speculated that this fellow with the Devil could have been the photographer. Hatfield's dress might dispel several of the myths that he was nothing more than a bloodthirsty, backwoods, hayseed hillbilly. Actually, by the time this photo was taken, Anse had earned a certain degree of wealth through land investments and timber businesses. He was a respected businessman in the region. — The collection of the West Virginia State Archives

THIS OLD photograph is believed to be Anderson "Devil Anse" Hatfield, or a close relative, when he was in his mid-30s. This is close to how Devil Anse would have looked as a member of the Wildcats militia. This photograph was found tucked away in the personal photograph album of his wife, Louvicey (Vicey) Chafin Hatfield. The resemblance is quickly apparent. — The Coleman C. Hatfield Collection

YOUNG JOE Hatfield poses behind the driver's seat in a Ford Model T touring. Passenger has not been identified.— The Coleman C. Hatfield Collection

JAMES (SLATER JIM) Hatfield, at left, was the uncle of Anse, whom a Civil War officer once ordered Anse to shoot because he briefly deserted the Confederate army. This prompted Anse to the leave the army by the end of 1863. Jim is shown with Rachel Toler.— The Coleman C. Hatfield Collection

WILLIS HATFIELD, a son of Anderson "Devil Anse" Hatfield, was in his late-70s by the time this snapshot was taken, above. He lived in a company house at a coal camp at Dehue, WV, during his final years. At left, a young Willis was once a deputy sheriff, along with several of his brothers, and was supposed to have been an exceptional pistol shot. — The Coleman C. Hatfield Collection

TOM WALLACE, shown in this photograph that has been oil painted and colorized, was Cap Hatfield's companion in the beating of the Daniels women, perhaps one of the most horrific episodes of the feud years. Tom was thought to have been killed in 1890, but it was later discovered he fathered one son in 1921. — The Coleman C. Hatfield Collection

THIS PHOTO, like the photograph on page 79, remains a mystery. No one really knows for sure when or where it was taken. The photographer is also unknown. Devil Anse appears to be around 75 years of age and has adopted a more formal, dapper style of dress. — The Coleman C. Hatfield Collection

IN HIS prime, Randal McCoy was the tough, determined, but tragic enemy of Devil Anse Hatfield. Some say he described Devil Anse as "six feet of devil and 180 pounds of hell." He had good reasons for thinking so because five of his children lost their lives to the bloody feud. Years before, Randal and Anse had been comrades during the War Between the States.

ROSEANNA McCOY is shown in this haunting photo when she was around 20 years old. She was once loved, but later abandoned by Johnse Hatfield. — The Coleman C. Hatfield Collection

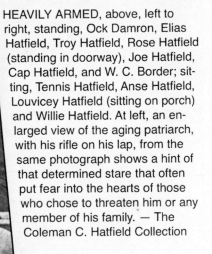

HEAVILY ARMED, above, left to right, standing, Ock Damron, Elias Hatfield, Troy Hatfield, Rose Hatfield (standing in doorway), Joe Hatfield, Cap Hatfield, and W. C. Border; sitting, Tennis Hatfield, Anse Hatfield, Louvicey Hatfield (sitting on porch) and Willie Hatfield. At left, an enlarged view of the aging patriarch, with his rifle on his lap, from the same photograph shows a hint of that determined stare that often put fear into the hearts of those who chose to threaten him or any member of his family. — The Coleman C. Hatfield Collection

THE TOWN of Aracoma, later named the City of Logan, was a small village when this photo was taken. The courthouse is in the center of the town, but there were not yet any churches in 1888.

PIKEVILLE, KENTUCKY is shown in this likeness. It was a town that was well known to Randal McCoy and his family as the place where their allies lived and worked.

NANCY VANCE Hatfield — Devil Anse's mother, Nancy, is shown here in her later years, holding probably a grandchild or great-grandchild, name unknown. A pioneer woman and hill country midwife, Nancy worried about Anse' well being during the feud years. — The Coleman C. Hatfield Collection

Above, Anderson "Devil Anse" and Louvicey Hatfield pose for the camera. Late in life, the Hatfields lived a peaceful existence. Below, the Hatfield family stands on their front porch at the home place at Sarah Ann. The photo includes Ossie Browning (granddaughter), Uncle Dyke Garrett (back row with white beard), and Rossie Browning (left). — The collection of the West Virginia State Archives

ANSE AND Louvicey are in the front of this family gathering with young Alie Hatfield, above; an unknown woman stands at left. In the back row is Tennis, Joe, Willis and Elizabeth Hatfield. At left, inset, Cap Hatfield, oldest son of Devil Anse, was one of the most violent and misunderstood of the feud participants. Below, left, Ellison (Cottontop) Mounts was the wood's colt son of Ellison Hatfield. Mounts was the only man executed by the Commonwealth of Kentucky in 1890. He confessed from the scaffold that he had indeed fired the shot that killed Allifair McCoy in the 1888 raid on the McCoy home. — The Coleman C. Hatfield Collection

THE DEVIL turned to stone, this photo shows the graveyard statue of the feud leader, surrounded by family members. In the center is grieving widow, Louvicey. Made of Italian marble, the statue lists the names of the thirteen children of Anderson and Louvicey Hatfield. The monument is still located at Sarah Ann, at the cemetery. — The Raamie Barker Collection

GRIEVING FAMILY and friends gathered at the Hatfield homeplace for the solemn occasion of Anderson "Devil Anse" Hatfield's funeral in January 1921. — The collection of the West Virginia State Archives

HUNDREDS OF friends and acquaintances gather at the Hatfield home, above, to mourn the passing of Devil Anse Hatfield. Below, besides the glare of the lens, this photo depicts the funeral service for Louvicey Chafin Hatfield. Her coffin leans forward for the photo, which was the custom of the times. She is surrounded by flowers, family and neighbors. — The collection of the West Virginia State Archives

JOHNSE HATFIELD was responsible for much trouble for the Hatfield clan. He had an undeniable "eye for the ladies" which often got him and others into trouble. For one, Johnse was involved with and soon abandoned Roseanna McCoy, who was pregnant with his child. — The Coleman C. Hatfield Collection

ASA HARMON (Bud) McCoy was one of the men who killed Jim Vance. He was a nephew of Ran'l McCoy. Bud was wounded in the fight at Grapevine Creek.— The collection of the West Virginia State Archives

CAMP STRATON — United Confederate Veterans members gathered for this photograph at a meeting near Chapmanville in 1901. The UVC charter ran Logan County politically for 40 years. Uncle William Dyke Garrett, with long white beard, is center in the first full row; Henry Clay Ragland, publisher of the local newspaper and historian, is in the second row, behind the man on Dyke Garrett's right.

HENRY CLAY Ragland, at left, was a lawyer, historian and journalist in Logan County. Ragland asserted his influence from his arrival in Logan in 1874 until his death in the spring of 1911. At right, Emma and Biddie Hatfield, two of Anse Hatfield's sisters, are shown in this photo.

CAP HATFIELD, oldest son of Devil Anse, sits and ponders the past at the rocky "panther site" on the mountainside. Cap was approximately 55 when this picture was taken. He was a county deputy and had also studied law by this time. — The Coleman C. Hatfield Collection

CAP HATFIELD stands in the center of this group of Logan County deputies, in front of the county courthouse. He was not a man to be reckoned with and was well-suited for law enforcement. — The Coleman C. Hatfield Collection

FRANK PHILLIPS, shown in this hand-colorized photograph, led the posse after the Hatfields and was involved in killing Jim Vance and fighting the battle of Grapevine Creek. — The collection of the West Virginia State Archives

DEVIL ANSE Hatfield finally made peace with his Maker and was baptized by Uncle Dyke Garrett in the chilly waters of Main Island Creek, near his home at Sarah Ann, WV, in October 1911. Even though it was a religious occasion, observers said he still packed a pistol in his pocket for protection. Sitting along the creek bank, on left, is Rev. Garrett, with beard. Below, left, Ellison Hatfield; right, Henry D. Hatfield became the most distinguished family member after the feud ended. He was a doctor, member of the McDowell County Court, governor and United States senator. — The collection of the West Virginia State Archives

ANSE POSED for an artist named Henry Craven when this photo was taken in 1911. A caption printed beneath this portrait in a *Life Magazine* feature claimed Anse was "rich and religious" when the photo was taken. That was likely true. — The collection of the West Virginia State Archives

ALLEN HATFIELD poses, at left, at a family get-together. At right, Allen and Willis stand together. — The Coleman C. Hatfield Collection

ANSE IS standing in the front row, the third man on the left, wearing hat, in this photograph of the Loyal Order Of Moose Lodge, Number 902, in Logan, WV. — The Coleman C. Hatfield Collection

COLEMAN A. Hatfield, grandson of Devil Anse and Hatfield family historian, posed for this snapshot on the Tug Fork River near War Eagle, around 1910. Inset, Coleman later became a respected attorney with a thriving legal practice in Logan, WV, developing an interest in law from his father, Cap. — The Coleman C. Hatfield Collection

THIS RARE photograph is of a bearded Ran'l McCoy in his elaborate coffin. He died on March 28th, 1914, from complications from falling into a fire. Devil Anse Hatfield lived until 1921.

COLEMAN C. Hatfield has been honored and recognized for his ongoing Hatfield family research. He passed away on January 14, 2008. — The Coleman C. Hatfield Collection

THIS STORE was owned and operated by Cap Hatfield and was located at Glen Alum. Through the years Cap owned several businesses, including saloons. — The Coleman C. Hatfield Collection

ANOTHER VIEW of the Devil Anse Hatfield homestead at Sarah Ann, this photo identifies the ginseng garden and spring house. Up the hill from this home is the location of the Hatfield cemetery. Unfortunately, the home no langer stands on the property. — The Coleman C. Hatfield Collection

THIS PHOTO of central Logan in 1895 is what the community resembled when the Anse Hatfield clan visited the county seat. — The Coleman C. Hatfield Collection

CAP HATFIELD, perhaps the most violent of the feud participants, poses at cliffside as a young man. History has proved that although Cap could be a violent man when pressured, he was interested in furthering his education. In middle-age, he earned his law degree and influenced his children to get a college education. — The Cole-

THIS LOG home, located at Holden, WV, near Logan, was situated on a busy logging camp that would have been similar in scope with Devil Anse Hatfield's first home and timber business in the Island Creek region of Logan County.

LEFT, DYKE Garrett, the pioneer preacher; right, an artist's depiction of Randall McCoy.

THE AGING Hatfield couple's photograph was taken around 1920. By this time, Anse had slowed down considerably. — The Coleman C. Hatfield Collection

ABOVE, RHODA and Bud McCoy on their wedding day, September 17, 1907. —
The collection of the West Virginia State Archives

ASA HARMON McCoy, brother of Randolph "Ran'l" McCoy. Asa, who enlisted in the Union Army, was brutally killed by Confederate supporters in 1865. Although some McCoy supporters held Devil Anse responsible, most students of the feud believe that his friend Jim Vance actually pulled the trigger. — The collection of the West Virginia State Archives

BUD AND Rhoda McCoy, photographed in 1944 (see their wedding day on page 142 in this volume). Bud was the grandson of Harmon McCoy, killed in the Civil War, and son of Lark McCoy, who played a leading part in the feud. — The collection of the West Virginia State Archives

JOHNSE HATFIELD and Roseanna McCoy are shown in this artist's depiction as young lovers, reprinted from *A Mountain Feud*. For years, writers have tried to portray the relationship between the two as an American version of the Romeo and Juliet story. Actually, the real story of Johnse and Roseanne was less idealistic. Roseanne was soon jilted by her Hatfield lover. — The collection of the West Virginia State Archives

These drawings from *A Mountain Feud* depict the battle between the families; bottom, right, this artwork is entitled, "Execution of the Three McCoy Boys," from *American Vendetta*. — The collection of the West Virginia State Archives

EXECUTION OF THE
THREE M'COY BOYS.

CAP HATFIELD (top photo, fourth from left) at a cave near Sarah Ann which served as a hideout during the feud. At left, Floyd Hatfield, cousin of Devil Anse, was accused by Randal McCoy of stealing a hog. Although a jury upheld Floyd Hatfield, his acquittal had been viewed by many as one of the precipitating factors of the Hatfield-McCoy feud. Below, Devil Anse' grandchildren: Jennings Harvey Howes and brother Lindsey Howes.— The collection of the West Virginia State Archives

DEVIL ANSE Hatfield, left, with brothers Ellison and Smith Hatfield. — The collection of the West Virginia State Archives

ED CHAMBERS and Sid Hatfield. Both men were killed on the steps of the McDowell County Courthouse on August 1, 1921. Sid, who was not related to Devil Anse, was a hero to coal miners due to his role in the Matewan Massacre. — The collection of the West Virginia State Archives

Attorneys Cap Hatfield and Joe Glenn. — The Coleman C. Hatfield Collection

CROCKETT HATFIELD plays with one of Devil Anse' pet bears, with an unidentified friend (some have suggested the man is Willis Hatfield). Below, the Red Top
Inn; Craig Hatfield, son of Bob, is standing second from right in the snapshot. — The
collection of the West Virginia State Archives

TENNIS AND Willis Hatfield, sons of Devil Anse, stand next to an unidentified woman. — The collection of the West Virginia State Archives

LOUVICEY AND Anse seem to ponder their lives at Sarah Ann. The couple saw much heartache over the years and depended greatly on one another in their old age. Below, left, Nancy Elizabeth Hatfield, Cap Hatfield's wife, and family gather around Louvicey, sitting, in her final years. Cap is standing at right. — The collection of the West Virginia State Archives and the Coleman C. Hatfield Collection

TOP, COLEMAN A. Hatfield and wife, Bertha "Mossy" Hatfield, were the proud parents of Coleman C. Hatfield, Aileen Hatfield, Christine Hatfield Lilly and Annabel Hatfield Goode. Below, left, Uncle Joe Hatfield and Evelyn Hatfield. Below, right, Cap, Nancy, and Cap's mother, Louvicey Hatfield. — The Coleman C. Hatfield Collection

A YOUNG Coleman A. Hatfield, top left, studied law and was concerned with documenting Hatfield history; and, right, this photo is of Coleman A. in later years as a respected attorney. Even though he was legally blind, he was still able to effectively practice law in Logan. Below, left, Cap poses in his Logan County deputy uniform. Below, right, a young Coleman Caldwell Hatfield, looks into the camera lens. The time was around 1934. — The Coleman C. Hatfield Collection

AT LEFT, Annabel Hatfield, grandaughter of Cap Hatfield and daughter of Mr. and Mrs. Coleman A. Hatfield, smiles while playing in the back yard in Logan, circa 1935.

Below, Coleman C. Hatfield with son, R. Mark Hatfield, and father Coleman A. Hatfield. — The Coleman C. Hatfield Collection

CAP AND Nan (Nancy Elizabeth Hatfield) pose with their children. This tattered photo was taken close to the most violent period of the feud. Cap was an imposing and dangerous figure who protected and defended his family in a variety of ways during the feud years. — The Coleman C. Hatfield Collection

JOE, TROY and Elias Hatfield, above, stand prepared with high-powered rifles. At left, Willis is heavily armed and intimidating as a deputy sheriff. Most the Hatfields were proficient with a variety of weapons, including billy-clubs, knives, rifles, shotguns and handguns. — The Coleman C. Hatfield Collection

ELIAS AND Tennis Hatfield, well-dressed, sit together in their younger days, above. Inset: Tennis with his family pose for the camera on their front porch.
— The Coleman C. Hatfield Collection

ABOVE, LARK and Mary Elizabeth McCoy. Below, McCoy relatives, left to right, Syler Branham, J.E. Stanley, and Joe Jack Stanley Jr. — The collection of the West Virginia State Archives

UNCLE DYKE and Sallie Smith Garrett posed for this photograph when Dyke was 70 years old. In many ways, he was the spiritual mentor to the Hatfield clan, and was especially close to Anse and Louvicey. — The Coleman C. Hatfield Collection

THE DEVIL'S preacher, Uncle Dyke Garrett, was called to preach the Gospel as a young adult. Over the years, he was extremely influential in building church congregations throughout Logan and Mingo County, in the mid-to-late 19th century. In this pose, Uncle Dyke holds the "Good Book" as he preaches the Good News of Jesus Christ. This original photograph hangs in the vestibule of the First Christian Church, on Stratton Street, Logan, WV. — Courtesy of the First Christian Church, Logan, WV

THE PATRIARCH, Devil Anse Hatfield — The Coleman C. Hatfield Collection

DEDICATION OF the Hatfield memorial at Anderson "Devil Anse" Hatfield's gravesite, in Sarah Ann, March 1922. The family cemetery is located up the hill from the location of the Devil Anse and Louvicey homeplace. Below, the Hatfield homestead, circa 1900. — The collection of the West Virginia State Archives

THE WILDCAT flag, in its worn state, is being preserved by the WV State Archives, in Charleston. Below, Ellison Hatfield's bloody pullover shirt. — The collection of the West Virginia State Archives

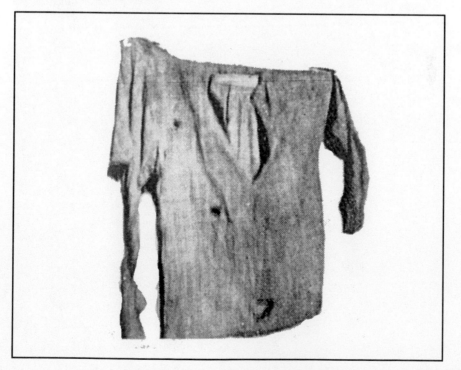

ARABEL HATFIELD, daughter of Coleman C. and Arthelia Bird Hatfield. Circa 1950s. At right, Coleman A. and Bertha "Mossy" Hatfield at their home. — The Coleman C. Hatfield Collection

Bertha Moss "Mossy" Caldwell Hatfield

MARY AND John Wongler, parents of Mrs. Henry D. Hatfield, whose husband was the grandson of Anse Hatfield. — The collection of the West Virginia State Archives

ON LEFT, CAP Glenn stands next to an aged Cap Hatfield, who is holding the leash to his pet fox. At right, Stewart Glenn also poses in the photo.

THIS PHOTO was first published nationally in *Life Magazine,* on May 22, 1944, of L. Lawson Hatfield. According to the account, Lawson squats inside an old hollow tree which was long known as the "stink tree," where Hatfields were said to have stuffed the dead bodies of their enemies. — Reprinted from *Life Magazine*

ALSO PUBLISHED in *Life Magazine*, on May 22, 1944, this is a photo of Joe D. Hatfield. Here he holds the shirt worn by his uncle Ellison on the day he was killed by three McCoys. There are 26 knife holes in the shirt. The three McCoys were killed the same day. Allegedly one of them, Little Randall, 15, was told to beg for his life but replied, "Go to hell!" He was then shot. — Reprinted from *Life Magazine*

HARK HATFIELD, 73, and his wife, Ollie McCoy Hatfield, pose for this photograph in a national publication, *Life Magazine*, as part of a feature entitled, *"Life Visits The Hatfields And McCoys."* — Reprinted from *Life Magazine*

FRANK McCOY stands on the swinging bridge leading to his home on Peter Creek. He has a gun in his hand but cautiously welcomed visitors at the time of this photo, taken in the 1940s. Frank married America Hatfield. — Reprinted from *Life Magazine*

DORNICK GRAVESTONE of Calvin McCoy, killed by Hatfields at the time of the "houseburning scrape." Dornicks are natural slabs of stone which are set up without aid of a professional stonecutter. Published on May 22, 1944. — Reprinted from *Life Magazine*

BUD McCOY and his wife, Rhoda McCoy, lived in this cottage beside Norfolk & Western railroad tracks. Below, a quilting bee in the home of Frank McCoy, Bud McCoy's brother. According to *Life Magazine,* two large stars in the upper corners are inscribed to the memory of Devil Anse Hatfield and Harmon McCoy. Photos published on May 22, 1944. — Reprinted from *Life Magazine*

HATFIELD KIDS (left) and McCoys (right) stage a tug-of-war in the yard of the Matewan school. Photos published on May 22, 1944. — Reprinted from *Life Magazine*

SHIRLEY HATFIELD, 17, left, and Mrs. Frankie McCoy Wellman worked together during World War II, making Army uniforms at Huntington, WV. Photo published on May 22, 1944.

— Reprinted from *Life Magazine*

RANDOLPH McCOY, at right, was an American pioneer and the proud patriarch of the McCoy family. The tall, broad-shouldered man, born October 30th, 1825, became a man of influence. He passed away on March 28th, 1914. It has been long reported that due to the family deaths, Randolph was never able to overcome his strong resentment toward the Hatfield family.

Bottom left, Joe "Uncle Joe" Hatfield poses in this rare snapshot; and bottom right, Glenn Hatfield is shown in this cabinet card. — The Coleman C. Hatfield Collection.

PAW PAW TREE INCIDENT

This episode is result of August 1882 election-day fight. Tolbert, a son of Randolph McCoy, exchanged heated words with Ellison Hatfield which started a fight. Tolbert, Pharmer and Randolph McCoy Jr. stabbed Ellison to death. Later the three brothers were captured by Hatfield clan, tied to pawpaw trees, and shot in retaliation.

Presented by Pikeville-Pike County Tourism

COLEMAN C. HATFIELD, above-left, meets with Kentucky Governor Paul E. Patton in 2003 to discuss Hatfield history. During the same year he met with Alabama and West Virginia's governors concerning preserving Hatfield and McCoy history. — Woodland Press

COLEMAN A. HATFIELD was an exceptional marksman as a young man. — The Coleman C. Hatfield Collection

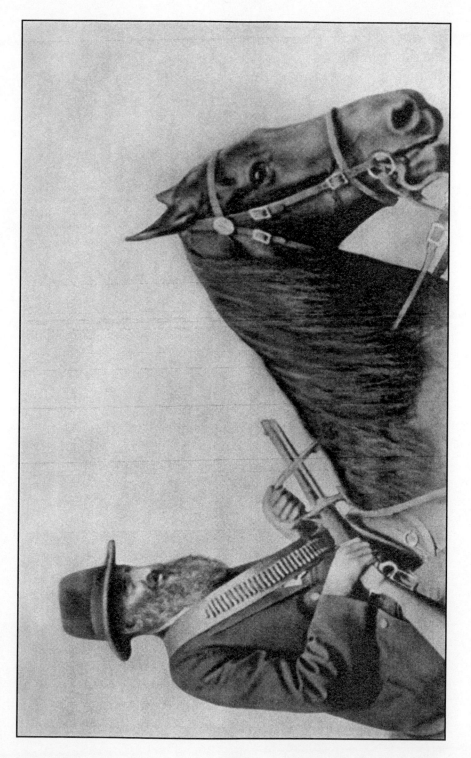

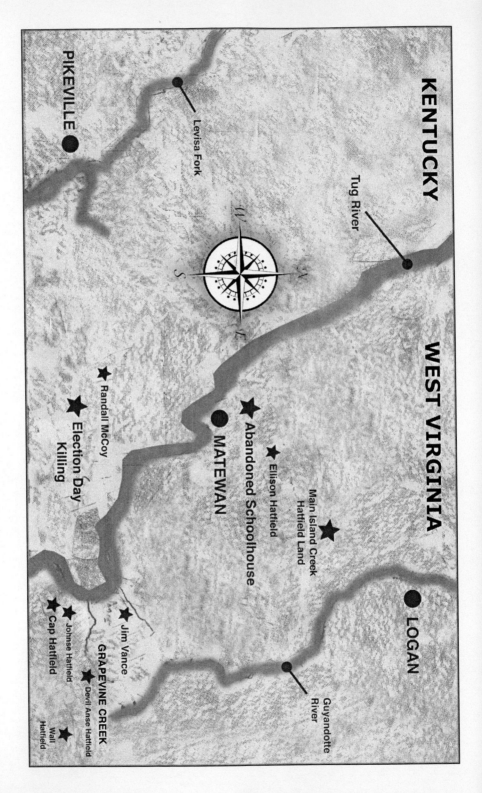

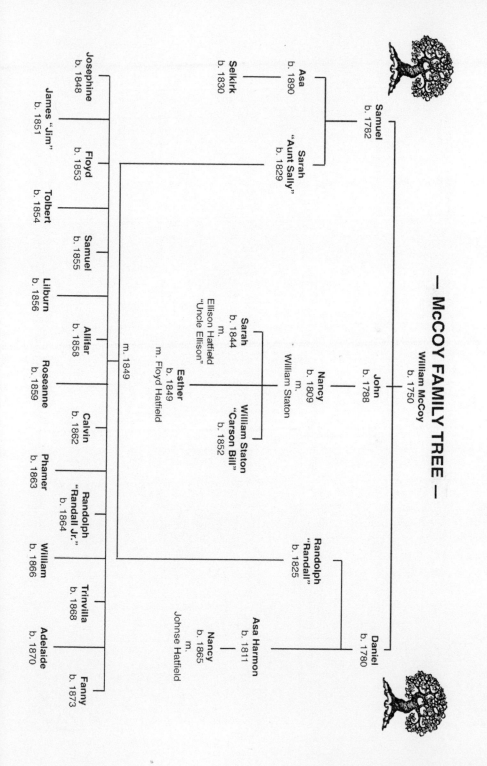

— McCOY FAMILY TREE —

William McCoy
b. 1750

Samuel
b. 1782

John
b. 1788

Daniel
b. 1780

Asa
b. 1890

Sarah
"Aunt Sally"
b. 1829

Nancy
b. 1809

Randolph
"Randall"
b. 1825

Asa Harmon
b. 1811

Selkirk
b. 1830

m.
William Staton

m. 1849

Sarah
b. 1844

m.
Ellison Hatfield
"Uncle Ellison"

Esther
b. 1849

m. Floyd Hatfield

William Staton
"Carson Bill"
b. 1852

Nancy
b. 1865

m.
Johnse Hatfield

Josephine
b. 1848

Floyd
b. 1853

Samuel
b. 1855

Alifiar
b. 1858

Calvin
b. 1862

Phamer
b. 1863

Randolph
"Randall Jr."
b. 1864

William
b. 1866

Trinvilla
b. 1868

Adelaide
b. 1870

James "Jim"
b. 1851

Tolbert
b. 1854

Liburn
b. 1856

Roseanne
b. 1859

Fanny
b. 1873

— HATFIELD FAMILY TREE —

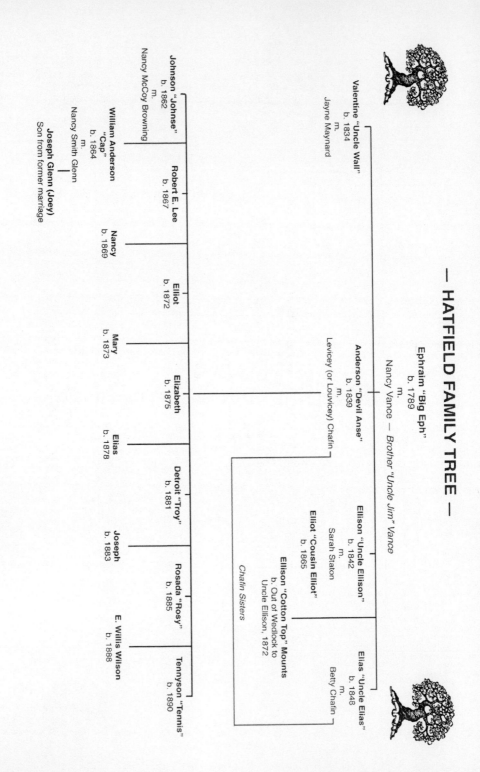

Ephraim "Big Eph"
b. 1789
m.
Nancy Vance — Brother "Uncle Jim" Vance

Valentine "Uncle Wall"
b. 1834
m.
Jayne Maynard

Anderson "Devil Anse"
b. 1839
m.
Levicey (or Louvicey) Chafin

Ellison "Uncle Ellison"
b. 1842
m.
Sarah Staton

Elias "Uncle Elias"
b. 1848
m.
Betty Chafin

Chafin Sisters

Johnson "Johnse"
b. 1862
m.
Nancy McCoy Browning

William Anderson
"Cap"
b. 1864
m.
Nancy Smith Glenn

Joseph Glenn (Joey)
Son from former marriage

Robert E. Lee
b. 1867

Nancy
b. 1869

Elliot
b. 1872

Mary
b. 1873

Elizabeth
b. 1875

Elias
b. 1878

Detroit "Troy"
b. 1881

Joseph
b. 1883

Rosada "Rosy"
b. 1885

E. Willis Wilson
b. 1888

Tennyson "Tennis"
b. 1890

Elliot "Cousin Elliot"
b. 1865

Ellison "Cotton Top" Mounts
b. Out of Wedlock to
Uncle Ellison, 1872

About The Feuding Hatfields & McCoys

The core of this manuscript, *The Feuding Hatfields & McCoys*, was first penned by Dr. Coleman C. Hatfield in 1978, to be used in conjunction with a television documentary. For one reason or another, the film was never made and the information was never published. It was in 2007 that Dr. Hatfield took a second look at the manuscript.

The original intent for the work was to be a "history at a glance" that would faithfully document Hatfield family migration and, in particular, give a timeline to the Hatfield and McCoy feud era. From the inception of the project, Dr. Hatfield credited a great deal of the historical information herein to his father, Coleman A. Hatfield. His father's meticulous research and documentation was used throughout this volume along with Dr. Hatfield's own study of the subject.

The following is a brief biographic sketch of Coleman A. Hatfield, written by his son, Dr. Hatfield:

Coleman A. Hatfield was once the chief family historian and a respected attorney in Logan. He spent much of his adult life carefully compiling Hatfield family stories and oral history.

C. A. Hatfield, as he was often called, was born in a log cabin at the mouth of Grapevine Creek in the north side of the Tug Fork of Sandy River on February 25, 1889, the eldest son of William Anderson (Cap) Hatfield and Nancy Elizabeth Hatfield, and the grandson of Anderson "Devil Anse" Hatfield.

The early life of C. A. Hatfield was spent in the log cabin home of his family on upper main Island Creek where he first attended school. His family later moved to Mingo County shortly after the railroad and mining development in the newly created county by that name. The family lived for a while at Baileysville, in Wyoming County.

At the age of fourteen, young Hatfield went to Concord School at Athens, West Virginia, were he finished in 1909. About that time he married tMossie Caldwell, having become acquainted with her as students in the institution from which they both graduated.

After graduation, he spent eight years in educational work and served as District Superintendent of Schools in one of the industrial districts of Mercer County.

Beginning January 1, 1917, he was connected with the Affiliated Lyceum Bureaus of America and was engaged in Lyceum and Chautauqua work where he traveled for more than a year over seventeen states throughout the Midwest and Southwest, including Oklahoma and Texas.

During the First World War, in the booming days of coal development on upper Island Creek, Hatfield was real estate agent and supervisor of buildings for Main Island Creek Coal Company, having within his duties the distribution of thousands of employees who came to that area during the industrial expansion of the company in the building of its plants at Micco, Chauncey, Omar, Barnabus and Stirrat.

In September, 1921, he entered West Virginia University Law School where he finished with the degree of Bachelor of Laws in 1924.

For the following 38 years he was engaged in the practice of law at Logan, where he was a member of the First Christian Church, Disciples of Christ, and a member of its official board.

In public service, he served two years as judge of the Municipal Court of the City of Logan and Divorce Commissioner of Logan County in the Seventh Judicial Circuit.

He spent his adult life documenting the history of the Hatfield family. His son, Dr. Coleman C. Hatfield, further researched the subject upon his father's passing in 1972.

Mr. and Mrs. Coleman A. Hatfield were the parents of Mrs. Leslie Lilly, Coleman C. Hatfield and Mrs. Claude A. Goode.

Thank You

A special thank you to the West Virginia Division Of Culture And History, and Commissioner Randall Reid-Smith, for the generosity and kind support that has been extended to the family of Dr. Coleman C. Hatfield and Woodland Press.

We would like to extend our deep appreciation for the use of the extensive Hatfield family photograph collection. Many of these historic photographs were initially donated to the State of West Virginia by the Coleman A. and Coleman C. Hatfield family along with their close relatives. Yet, it remains a wonderful gesture on the part of the Division Of Culture And History to allow us this opportunity to publish selections from this special historical collection.

Also, we want to thank Dr. R. Mark Hatfield and Dr. Arabel Hatfield for their kindnesses, support and commitment to this project. Also, our deepest gratitude to the support and assistance of Raamie Barker and Cheryl R. Davis.

A special thanks to West Virginia Governor Earl Ray Tomblin for his constant encouragement and support of projects like this that faithfully document Mountain State history, and to U.S. Senator Joe Manchin and U.S. Congressman Nick Rahall for supporting the preservation of southern West Virginia history.

About the Authors

Dr. Coleman C. Hatfield: a uniquely talented, creative and brilliant man. Storyteller, author and historian, Dr. Hatfield unexpectedly passed away on Monday, January 14th, 2008, at age 81, when this literary project was being finalized. He was born in Logan, West Virginia, on September 25, 1926.

Coleman was not only a noted historian, writer and president of Hatfield Historical Associates, he was also a dedicated optometrist, genealogist, gemologist, botanist, bee-keeper and storyteller.

A true Hatfield, he loaded his own ammo and was a master with a pistol or rifle on a target range.

He was an *exceptionally* learned man who was passionate about many things, including the preservation of Hatfield family history.

Coleman graduated from Logan High School, Concord University, and Illinois College of Optometry. At Illinois College of Optometry he was a professor and chairman of the vision therapy and children's clinic. He was also the author of the vision therapy book, *The Joy of Optometry.*

He served as president of the West Virginia Optometric Association and was a member of the examination board of the College of Optometrists in Vision Development. He practiced optometry in both Chicago and Logan with his daughter, Dr. Arabel E. Hatfield, and son, Dr. R. Mark Hatfield, until his retirement.

As a writer and historian, Coleman was named West Virginia Author of the Year, a prestigious award presented by Tamarack-The Best of West Virginia for his biography, *The Tale of the Devil*, about his great-grandfather, Anderson "Devil Anse" Hatfield.

Over the last few years he presented signed copies of the book to several acting and former governors in West Virginia, Kentucky and Alabama, and other dignitaries. He spoke with each of them of the importance of preserving family history. In a real way, he was the goodwill ambassador for the Hatfield family.

He was a Christian statesman, active in the First Christian Church of Logan and the Hometown Christian Church in Chicago. He taught a Men's Bible class and served as an elder and trustee.

Coleman had a wonderful zest for life and learning — and was a well-rounded individual — with a *dynamic* sense of humor and quick wit. He was admired by many who knew him.

During the last years of his life he was planning and working on another major project, a biography about his grandfather, Cap

Hatfield, second son of Anderson "Devil Anse" Hatfield. The project was tentatively to be called *The Devil's Advocate: The Biography Of Cap Hatfield*.

Coleman told me story after story over the years that were to be included in the finished manuscript. He had mentally plotted out the chapters and knew exactly what he wanted to achieve with his writings. Had he completed the work, it would have been wonderful. — *By F. Keith Davis*

* * *

Co-author F. Keith Davis is a longtime Mountain State newspaperman and independent book publisher who has held a variety of roles over the last thirty years, including graphic designer, journalist, newspaper general manager and publisher. With this project, his role was to edit and adapt the manuscript accordingly, while preserving Dr. Hatfield's distinct voice.

Davis is a lifelong student of American history and especially enjoys researching southern West Virginia's colorful past. His titles include *The Secret Life and Brutal Death of Mamie Thurman*, *West Virginia Tough Boys*, *Images of America: Logan County*, and *After All These Years: The Authorized Biography of the Hoppers*.

He has written articles for, or been recognized by, a number of publications including *West Virginia Magazine*, *Goldenseal Magazine*, *West Virginia Executive* and various newspapers across the country. He has penned features for *Singing News Magazine*, *U.S. Gospel News*, *Bill & Gloria Gaither's Homecoming Magazine* and numerous history-based and inspirational websites, as well.

As an author and historian, Keith has been interviewed or featured for programs airing on The History Channel, C-Span BookTV, The 700 Club, WV Public Television and Radio, Metronews Talkline with Hoppy Kercheval, Viewpoint with Jean Dean, FOX News, and elsewhere.

He is the CEO of Woodland Press, LLC, a small, independent book publishing firm that focuses on Appalachian-based book titles.

Keith resides with his wife, Cheryl, and family in Chapmanville, WV.

THE DEVIL'S SON
Cap Hatfield and the End
Of the Hatfield and McCoy Feud
ANNE BLACK GRAY
FOREWORD BY G. CAMERON FULLER

The Devil's Son
Cap Hatfield and the End of the Hatfield and McCoy Feud
BY ANNE BLACK GRAY

You think you know who they were, why they fought, why they died. You know only the legend—now experience the real feud. *The Devil's Son*, published by Woodland Press, is a vast historical epic that breathes life into the individuals and families on either side of the Tug River. At the center of the tale is Cap Hatfield, son of Devil Anse, the seminal figure in the feud. While the battle rages, Cap wrestles with coming of age in the shadow of the Devil. Featured as resource material in the 2012 nationally televised documentary on the Hatfield-McCoy Feud. —Softcover. 352 Pages.

> "Never before has an author so vividly captured the drama, action and character of what stands as America's most famous feud. Anne Black Gray has dared to step beyond the "legend" surrounding the Hatfields & McCoys. THE DEVIL'S SON now stands as the benchmark book on this subject." **—Mark Cowen**, director/producer, Emmy®-nominated HBO documentary, BAND OF BROTHERS: We Stand Alone Together.

www.woodlandpress.com

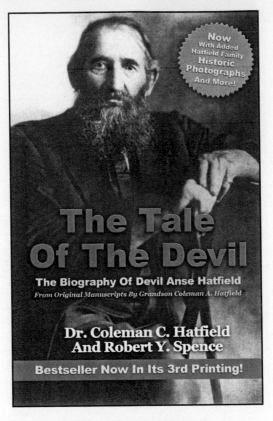

Now With Added Hatfield Family Historic Photographs And More!

The Tale Of The Devil
The Biography Of Devil Anse Hatfield
From Original Manuscripts By Grandson Coleman A. Hatfield

Dr. Coleman C. Hatfield
And Robert Y. Spence

Bestseller Now In Its 3rd Printing!

Tale of the Devil
The Biography of Devil Anse Hatfield

BY DR. COLEMAN C. HATFIELD and ROBERT Y. SPENCE

The first biography of Anderson "Devil Anse" Hatfield, penned by great-grandson Dr. Coleman C. Hatfield and Mountain State historian Robert Y. Spence. *Tale of the Devil* is the story of the Hatfield family patriarch. It covers his service in the Civil War with the Wildcats and features in-depth coverage of the feud years, as well as the era after the gunfire ceased. — Hardback. 320 Pages.

This collaborative effort of Coleman C. Hatfield and Robert Y. Spence, *The Tale Of The Devil,* is the factual biography of Devil Anse Hatfield, and the role he played in the infamous and brutal Hatfield and McCoy feud. Coleman Hatfield is Devil Anse Hatfield's direct descendant and brings a special and personal expertise to this project. *The Tale Of The Devil* candidly examines this figure's early life, the origins of the Hatfield and McCoy feud, its brutal toll, denouement, and ultimate conclusion — as well as the impact it has had on subsequent generations of Hatfields and McCoys. A profound, sometimes dark, yet often insightful life story, *The Tale Of The Devil* is a very highly recommended addition to American History and Biography collections. —**Midwest Book Review**

www.woodlandpress.com

FULL BONE MOON

BY G. CAMERON FULLER

Someone is killing West Virginia University students. Again. Six years ago, two WVU freshmen were last seen hitchhiking back to their dorms after seeing a movie in downtown Morgantown. Their bodies were later found in the dark woods south of town. E.P. Clawson was convicted of the murders, but Michael Chase, a reporter for the *Herald-Dispatch*, never thought Clawson was guilty—a belief that nearly cost him his career. Now the murders have started again. Female WVU students are disappearing, and their defiled bodies are found with ritual markings. Full Bone Moon, a first place winner, novel, in the annual West Virginia Writers contest, follows Michael Chase as he tracks the ritual killers through the streets, underground tunnels, and forests of Morgantown. Inspired by the actual murders of Mared Malarik and Karen Ferrell in Morgantown in 1970, Full Bone Moon employs the many rumors and speculation that swirled around the Morgantown area after the killings, and continue to this day. Rumors of cult activity, high society complicity, police corruption and coverup, and FBI treachery are woven together in Full Bone Moon to take you on a wild ride—a fast-paced fictional thriller—through the Coed Murders as they could have happened. —Softcover. 276 Pages.

> "Full Bone Moon is a bona fide gut-wrencher. Dark, smart, and quite honestly impossible to put down at three o'clock in the morning! G. Cameron Fuller shows us this gritty tale through the light of a full bone moon . . . and dares us to blink."
> — **Michael Knost**, Bram Stoker Award-Winner

w w w . w o o d l a n d p r e s s . c o m

Stories from the Hearth
Heartwarming Stories of Appalachia
EDITED BY BRIAN J. HATCHER

New stories with deep roots. Experience the power of Appalachian storytelling as twelve exceptional authors from around the world give their unique interpretations on a truly unique art form. Local, national and international voices honor a grand tradition by telling stories as fresh as a mountain stream and as old as the hills. Powerful tales to edify the mind, move the heart and stir the soul.

In this anthology, you'll find powerful stories by Beth Cato, Diane Tarantini, Shelly Li, Karin Fuller, Rachel Towns, Jamie Lackey, Lee Ann Sontheimer Murphy, Josh Reynolds, Theodore Carter, Jeff Baker, Steve Rasnic Tem and Sara J. Larson. —Softcover. 128 Pages.

www.woodlandpress.com

Other Great Titles
By Woodland Press, LLC

**The Secret Life and Brutal Death
Of Mamie Thurman**
F. Keith Davis

Legends of the Mountain State
Ghostly Tales from the State of West Virginia
Edited by Michael Knost

Legends of the Mountain State 2
More Ghostly Tales from the State of West Virginia
Edited by Michael Knost
Foreword by U.S. Senator Joe Manchin, III

Legends of the Mountain State 3
More Ghostly Tales from the State of West Virginia
Edited by Michael Knost
Foreword by Homer Hickam

Legends of the Mountain State 4
More Ghostly Tales from the State of West Virginia
Edited by Michael Knost

Writers Workshop of Horror
—Winner of the 2009 Bram Stoker Award—
Edited by Michael Knost

Arch: The Life of WV Gov. Arch A. Moore, Jr.
Brad Crouser

Blair Mountain War, Battle of the Rednecks
G.T. Swain

Princess Aracoma
G.T. Swain

West Virginia Tough Boys
F. Keith Davis
Foreword by WV Gov. Earl Ray Tomblin

The Mothman Files
Edited by Michael Knost
Foreword by Jeff Wamsley
Afterword By Thomas F. Monteleone

Shadows and Mountains:
Jessie Grayson and Ellen Thompson McCloud

Mountain Magic
Edited by Brian J. Hatcher
Foreword by Lucy A. Snyder

"The hills and valleys that once rang with the report of pistols and rifles, and whose soil was bathed with human blood, is now stilled in peace."

— G.T. Swain, 1927

Woodland Press, LLC

CPSIA information can be obtained at www.ICGtesting.com
Printed in the USA
LVOW092201310512

284191LV00002B/9/P